ST. PAUL THE APOSTLE

The Right Man at the Right Time

3rd Edition

ST. PAUL THE APOSTLE

The Right Man at the Right Time

3rd Edition

Irving L. Brittle Jr.

THE REGENCY
PUBLISHERS

ISBN: 978-1-957724-65-2 (Paperback Edition)
ISBN: 978-1-957724-64-5 (Hardcover Edition)
ISBN: 978-1-957724-66-9 (E-book Edition)

Book Ordering Information

Phone Number: 315 288-7939 ext. 1000 or 347-901-4920
Email: info@theregencypublishers.com
The Regency Publishers
www.theregencypublishers.com

Printed in the United States of America

Contents

DEDICATION

My Wife, Sue King Brittle, My Daughter Ashton Leigh Freeman, and Grandson Ryder Luke Freeman

My Parents Irving L. Brittle, Sr, My Mother Helen Patz Brittle My Sister Linda B. Kines, whose Support and Financial Assistance Made My Two Books Possible

Dr. Charles Stanley

Staff and Technical Persons at Pen House Publishing LLC, Sheridan, WY: Special thanks to Anna Cortez

My New Friends and Fellow Members at First Baptist Clermont, Clermont Florida

Dallas Theological Seminary, Dallas, Texas

PREFACE

St. Paul the Apostle, 3rd Edition, has been an ongoing work for over eight years, and   this "Third Edition" will be my last. The purpose of the Third Edition titled **St. Paul the Apostle: The Right Man at the Right Time** is again to include new information, rearrange several chapters at the suggestions of those whose opinions I respect, and to 'do more justice to St. Paul the Apostle.'

In 2013, I determined I was going to read the Bible - cover to cover. But I found that was not enough; I had to 'study' the Bible if I was going to receive a true meaning of God's Word in the Old and New Testaments. I got 'stuck' in the Book of Acts with-and when a man named Paul of Tarsus captured my attention and has ever since. Next to Jesus Christ in the New Testament, St. Paul was the Christian who can arguably be the most influential person in the New Testament. After his encounter with the 'living Christ on the Damascus road,' his 'appointment and charge from Christ' as the man to spread the Gospel of Jesus Christ to both Gentiles and the Jews, and his new theology of Christ written into his many Epistles to churches in the Roman Empire, there is much to absorb.

St. Paul was a very complex man with a history and life worthy of further study from theological and historical perspectives. He was 'the foot soldier' in charge of spreading this new religion, originally known as 'the Way;' later the followers were called Christians. Interestingly, this directive from Christ ran counter to everything Paul believed earlier in his life as a devout Jew and 'Zealous Pharisee.'

When reading through the book and learning the many aspects of Paul's life, you will appreciate Paul as a very resilient, strong, strong-willed man who never lost sight of his mission to spread the Gospel of Jesus Christ. Paul, on several occasions faced execution for his new beliefs. One of many ways he spread his new gospel of Christ was through his writings (Epistles). Paul was a prolific writer as evidenced by his thirteen Epistles in the New Testament.

As in the first-three editions of **St. Paul the Apostle,** I have tried to keep the information and story '*basic*,' a polished mosaic, again with the hope that someone may use the book to teach a Sunday School class on St. Paul. I did not want a book 'loaded with facts,' but there are thousands of sources about Paul; what you read in the book is a 'small tip of the iceberg' on the life of St. Paul.

The book is in a sense a 'shotgun approach and panorama' of the fascinating story of St. Paul (as I believe I know him), his Epistles, and with a 'touch' of his theology as it developed (the exception is the chapter on the Book of Romans). The book is duly footnoted with scripture and verses directly from the Bible – the Word of God – hard to argue with the Bible! You will also find 'Study Questions' at the end of the chapters to help focus on the main facts I am trying to convey.

I have authored a second book, third edition, **It's Not Rocket Science: The Theology of St. Paul** that addresses his theology, and again based on scripture. If you desire to further your study of St. Paul, please refer to the Bibliography and the many 'Biblical academicians, scholars, and theologians' who have dedicated their entire lives to the life and works of St. Paul.

Welcome to the Life of

St. Paul the Apostle:

The Right Man at the Right Time

INTRODUCTION

St. Paul the Apostle: The Right Man at the Right Time is a biography-autobiography, commentary, narrative with dialogue straight from St. Paul as St. Luke 'wrote and recorded' in the Book of Acts – '*a historical story.*' Paul 'earned' the title 'Apostle to the Gentiles,' and how he earned the title is a full, rich, challenging, and multifaceted story; one that included a questionable early life and a career as a Zealot, *a Zealot Pharisee.*

The chronology of events and history that occurred during Paul's lifetime is as specific as can be determined through historical, biographical, and biblical data. It was interesting to unearth new and relevant historical information concerning his life and death; for instance, the parents of Jesus Christ and the parents of Paul 'may' have lived within miles of each other when each was born.

The book is amply footnoted, including footnotes specifying Biblical verses adding to the 'where abouts' of Paul during specific times and years of his life. The footnotes are also '*a treasure trove*' of authors who can help you 'dig deeper' into specific times and events in Paul's life; my hope is you consider doing just that.

St. Paul the Apostle is also a book of '*hope.*' St. Paul's entire life was built on the hope people he reached would listen to the Gospel of Jesus Christ and respond in faith especially after his Damascus road experience. The times between the Damascus road event and St. Paul's final years in prison in Rome frames the true story of the man whose entire life was purpose driven with an underlying 'hope' he would effectively spread the Gospel of Christ to the Jews and Gentiles of that era.

Paul was not just another *'idle babbling prophet,'* as Epicurean and Stoic philosophers flippantly remarked in Athens and *'certainly not out of his mind'* when questioned by Festus and Herod Agrippa II during his trials in Caesarea before being sent off to Rome to be tried before Caesar (Nero). Paul was a man of deep conviction whose life and thought processes were *'radically'* changed from a Zealous Pharisee to St. Paul the 'Apostle to the Gentiles' over an approximately 30+ year period.

A question often arises as to whether Paul was a *theologian, a missionary, or pastor.* The implicit answer to the question is – *'yes to all three.'* St. Luke's Book of Acts and Paul's Epistles provide us with a portrait of a *"warm-hearted pastor, insightful theologian, and passionate evangelist."*

One of my favorite and early descriptions of St. Paul's personality was written in the book by Thomas D. Lea and David Alan Black titled *The New Testament: It's Background and Message*:

> "Paul's personality was as varied and sparkling as a multifaceted diamond. In matters of doctrinal importance, he could be as unbending as hardened steel. In debatable issues he was pliable as rubber.

> His relationships with his churches alternated between supportive love and strong, but compassionate rebuke. Paul's love for his converts shines brilliantly in each of his letters.

> His will could be unyielding under pressure, he was not easily discouraged, nor did trials fill him with self-pity."

You will find St. Paul had amazing physical stamina. When not traveling by boat, *'he walked'* – thousands of miles over the course of his three missions (possibly six). During his first mission, he visited the city of Lystra in Asia Minor. There were those in Lystra (Judaizers) who did not embellish his new Gospel of Christ, and he was dragged from the city and stoned – *'left for dead.'* Of course, he recovered and never easily deterred, he stayed in Lystra another day, and left for Derbe with his companion Barnabas. Again, he visited the city later during his first mission and during his second mission.

During my time in writing St. Paul the Apostle, I was asked on several occasions, *"What did Paul 'look like?'"* From pictures and statues, one might assume he was tall; some representations had him with long hair, some bald, often armed with a sword. There is no physical description of Paul in any version of contemporary Bibles I researched.

I did find a story in *The Lost Books of the Bible and Forgotten Books of Eden* about Paul and one of his disciples and followers, *Thecla,* that may provide a clue. Many of the early third and fourth century writers back the story as true and original such as *Cyprian,* a Christian theologian and bishop of Carthage later to be the first Bishop martyred in Africa in 258 AD. Another was *Eusebius,* a learned scholar who lived most likely in Caesarea in Palestine. His greatest contribution is *Historia Ecclesiastica* (Church History), and extensive history of the Christian Church from the time of the apostles until AD 323. There were also *Epiphanius* and *Sulpicius Severus,* both fourth-century ecclesiastical writers.

The Lost Books of the Bible and Forgotten Books of Eden is not considered one of the original books of early Christianity. It is published from a Greek MS (review) in the Bodleian Library at Oxford and was copied, translated, and transmitted to Dr. Grabe at Oxford.

'Thecla became a disciple of the early Christian church and was a student and follower of St. Paul in Asia Minor.' Consider the following verses from the chapter entitled *"The Acts of Paul and Thecla:"*

> "And a certain man named Onesiphorus, hearing that Paul was coming to Iconium, went out speedily to meet him together with his wife Lectra, and his sons Simmia and Zeno, to invite him to their home.

> For Titus had provided them a description of Paul's personage, they, as yet, not knowing him in person but only being acquainted with his character.

> They went to the king's highway to Lystra, and stood there waiting for him, comparing all who passed-by with a description which Titus had provided.

> At length they saw a man coming [namely Paul], of a low stature, bald (or shaved head), crooked thighs, handsome legs, hollowed-eyed, had a crooked nose, full of grace; for sometimes he appeared as a man, sometimes he had the countenance of an angel. And Paul saw Onesiphorus and was glad.

> And Onesiphorus said: 'Hail, thou servant of the blessed God.' Paul replied, 'The grace of God be with thee and thy family.'"

Paul was the most significant missionary in the history of the early Christian church. He brought to his missionary task an intense fearless driving personality with a commitment to, and faith in Jesus Christ. As one further studies the life of St. Paul, it becomes evident that he was centered-in and walked in Christ (Christocentric), and Paul as formerly mentioned, almost lost his life on several occasions due to his *'fearlessness and never backing down'* from his newfound belief and faith in Jesus Christ. As a new Christian in the Roman era, he certainly had his fair share of *'trials and tribulations.'* He was jailed seven times during his ministry, beaten, and often simply "run out of cities" where he delivered his message, often by his fellow Jews.

Paul was a man of enormous physical and mental stamina. He faced many hardships and court-like trials, as expressed in the letters to his churches and his closest companions. *"His ability to withstand this variety of rigorous experiences testifies to his resilience and durability."* He learned the skills of being content amid the extremes of both poverty and plenty.

Paul could function tactfully in various delicate situations, when he discussed the subject of *'giving' ('the collection'* for the impoverished Jews in Judea) with the Corinthian Christian church. His flexibility did not indicate weakness as he attempted to understand the viewpoints of the believers. In his personal relationships, Paul maintained his principles without showing deceit.

Paul aimed his fiercest outbursts at those who tried to mislead his converts and fired vehement rebukes at Jewish legalists (Judaizers) who attempted to underhandedly mislead Christians into following all aspects of the Jewish law as 'the means of and only way to salvation.' He spoke forcefully, and firmly, to any who willfully tried 'to turn' new Christian coverts from their newfound commitment to Jesus Christ and the Gospel.

Three years after his conversion (transformation) to Christ on the Damascus road, Paul had to not only convince the original twelve disciples in Jerusalem of his faith and belief in Christ, he had to convince the many who knew him formally as a zealot Pharisee and ardent enemy of the new faith and believers of 'the Way.'

If you're a 'book browser' and read only the Preface and Introduction – you may wish to congratulate yourself. Even with this brief introduction, you can say, 'I know more information on St. Paul the Apostle than approximately 50% of all church goer's including those Christians committed to faith in Jesus Christ as their Lord and Savior.'

When I first started the works on St. Paul, I questioned many people and asked, 'what do you know about St. Paul?' Some had never heard of him, most remembered hearing his name during church services, and others didn't care who he was – sad; there were those who could have taught me a thing or two.

If you're a Christian, or non-Christian, keep reading and enjoy 'the story' of the man and his close companions (Barnabas, Mark, Timothy, Titus, St. Luke, and others) who we say, 'pioneered early Christianity.' **St. Paul the Apostle: The Right Man at the Right Time-Third Edition** is first, and foremost, a historical story, 'a snapshot' of an extensive, magnificent biography of 'God's chosen servant, commissioned to spread the Gospel, and bring Jesus Christ into the lives of those followers in his era (and ours), and teach us we can have eternal life in heaven by a belief and faith in Christ.'

If you wish to learn more about Paul's theology, please consider reading my book It's Not Rocket Science: The Theology of St. Paul-Third Edition. One goal in writing the books was to offer 'basic' knowledge of the apostle, and if so inspired, please teach a Sunday School class on St. Paul. I have a website (**www.irvingbrittlebooks.com**) and email (sonnybrittle3@gmail.com) where you may contact me, and I have written a syllabus for such an endeavor (you can make your own).

A *PowerPoint* presentation is in the works (I will be able to download and email the attachment). My hope is you enjoy reading the story of St. Paul as much as I have been thinking, writing, and researching- and having the results published. God be with You, and 'Walk in the light.'

THE ROMAN EMPIRE IN THE DAYS OF ST. PAUL AND BEFORE

At the peak of its expansion, Rome controlled 2.3 million square miles of land encompassing the Mediterranean Sea. The Empire existed between 753 BC and AD 800. From AD 800 until 1806, much of the area was known as the Holy Roman Empire. To a degree, Roman rule brought peace to this part of the world. During this time within the Roman Empire many architectural structures were built and exist to this day. The foundation of the city of Rome was laid in 550 BC. Paul's birth is dated between 5 BC and AD 5 (Jesus and Paul were very close in age); Paul's missions occurred between AD 47-49 through AD 54-58 (59). The dates recorded for Paul's birth and his missionary journeys literally run-the gamut; for instance, one record has his birth at 2 BC, another at AD 10. The above mission dates are close. There were dated occurrences in-and around Judea at the time that may have led extant researches to estimate the dates, especially of his missions; Paul's birth was recorded in Rome-no date given.

People and civilizations conquered by Rome, especially the Jews of Palestine, resented Roman occupation and the cruelty of the

Roman soldiers and satellite-Roman governments set-up in these territories.

St. Paul and the early Christians found benefits living in the Roman Empire, for instance:

- Initial Roman government tolerance for Christianity trumped Jewish leaders (Pharisees, Sadducees, and *Judaizers*) persecution of Christians. Good examples specific to St. Paul occurred on several occasions when Jewish legalists (*Judaizers*) attempted to try and sentence Paul to an early death. Paul had a *Roman citizen's right to legally defend* himself on more than one occasion.

In a personal defense of his character and his views before the Roman officials Festus and Herod Agrippa II (after his third mission) in the Roman province of Caesarea, Paul won an appeal that should have granted him a hearing before Caesar (Nero) in Rome – a trip to Rome, all expenses paid.[1] The sea voyage (AD 60-61) to Rome almost cost him his life as did the 'stoning in Lystra during his first mission' – 'trials and tribulations!!!

- Roman infrastructure aided early Christianity with its vast network of roads (some paved) known a *Via's,* and civil institutions allowed Christians to travel within the Roman Empire quickly, without hindrances and often 'bandit free.'

- The Roman peace (*Pax Romana*) occurring between 27 BC and AD 180 meant the empire was not involved in major wars. Christians traveled safely and freely by land and sea without concerns of getting 'caught up in armed

---

[1] Stanley, *Life Principles Bible, Acts 25:13; 26:32.*

conflicts.' The missionary journeys of Paul demonstrated this freedom of movement. Paul could choose to go and end his journeys in densely populated cities that provided large audiences for his Christian messages (Thessalonica, Athens Corinth, Ephesus, Rome).

- *Kione* Greek[2] was a common language that essentially united the Eastern and Western Roman Empire dialect. People in different areas held on to their local dialects, but *Kione* Greek became a universally understood language in the Roman Empire. Many of the New Testament Epistles were written and distributed in this common language of the time allowing relatively quick dissemination and understanding of St. Paul's Epistles and theology.

- Even though the Roman government eventually turned hostile to Christianity from the time of Nero (AD 54) until Constantine (AD 313), early decades of peace allowed Orthodox Christianity to grow and spread. But in other areas Christians still had to hide or run for their lives.

'In many and various ways, God of old spoke to our fathers by the prophets, but in the last days He has spoken to us by a Son, whom He appointed the heir of things, through whom also He created the ages.'[3]

And his Son, Christ, commanded His disciples: "Go . . . And you shall be My witnesses in Jerusalem and in all Judea and Samaria and to the ends of the earth."[4]

---

[2] "Kione Greek," *Wikipedia, last modified April 3, 2017, accessed April 3, 2017,* https://en.wikipedia.org/wiki/Kione Greek.

[3] Stanley, *Life Principles Bible, Hebrews 1:1,2.*

[4] Stanley, *Life Principles Bible, Acts 1:8.*

The dispersion (Diaspora) of the Jewish population was caused by periods of migration and in other cases by conquest placing groups of Jewish people in captivity. From 800 BC to 567 BC, many Jews in Palestine took refuge in Egypt. In 567 BC, Nebuchadnezzar captured Jerusalem, also capturing and *destroying* the temple. A mass deportation ensued, bringing a new influx of refugees into the land of the Nile.

Over time, there developed differences between the Jews of the East Diaspora and Jews of the West Diaspora. Though in division, they worshipped the one God; as time progressed, their language and written documents differed. Those of the East communicated in Greek, Hebrew and Aramaic, and the Jews of the West Diaspora likely spoke more Greek and Latin in the territories lying from Greece westward to Italy; over time the differences increased.[5]

Even though the conquests by Alexander the Great occurred years before the birth of Christ (approximately 335 BC), Alexander was instrumental in the spread of Christianity. His ambition was to gather all nations and make a united world. After Alexander's conquests, Greek was *nearly* the primary dialect in the entire ancient East. Alexander succeeded in that Greek became the common language all around the Mediterranean as far as Marseilles (France) and the Pillars of Hercules (eastern end of the Strait of Gibraltar), and the books of the Old Testament were translated into Greek for the benefit of the Hellenized Jews in the city of Alexandria, Egypt.

The letters of Paul were mostly written in Greek as was the rest of the New Testament. Christian missionaries could express themselves in this language wherever the Spirit led them without having concerns about speaking the various languages of the regions they visited during Paul's life and after his death.

[5] Doron Mendels, "Why Paul Went West," accessed April 2, 2014, *Archaeology Review 371 (January/February 2011): 49-54, 68,* http://members.bib-arch.org/biblical-archaeolgy review/3722/20.

Closer to Paul's era, the Syrian king Antiochus IV Epiphanes ruled in the territories in and around Israel between 174 BC and 164 BC. He proved no friend of the Jews, and again there were mass migrations that populated the entire coast of Asia Minor with immigrants; many were Jews from Palestine and Babylon. Antiochus mounted efforts to destroy the Jews, their way of life, religion, and the temple. Jews praying to their God on the Sabbath was deemed a capital offense. Antiochus scourged the area, killing Jewish mothers and their circumcised babies. Estimates are as high as eighty thousand Jews lost their lives while he ruled Judea.

Antiochus committed his greatest and most egregious outrage by entering the temple, erecting an altar to Zeus, and slaughtering a pig as a sacrifice. *That desecration*, considered by the Jews to be *an abomination*, occurred on the twenty-fifth of Kislev, according to the *Bible Calendar* (167 BC). His actions triggered the Maccabean Revolt by the Hasmoneans in 167-to 63 BC.

The Maccabees' victory and cleansing of the temple is still commemorated by Jews today and is known as the ***Annual Festival of Hanukkah***. According to Jewish tradition, at the time of the rededication of the temple, there was not enough lamp oil for the *menorah* in the temple which was to burn continuously each night. Miraculously, a single day supply of oil burned for eight days until fresh oil became available; this eight-day festival initiated the commemoration of the miracle that continues to this day.[6]

In 63 BC, Pompey, a famous Roman general, brought a contingent of Jews as captives to Rome. Later, these *Romanized Jews* provided Julius Caesar with funds to help him rise to power. In return, in 47 BC Julius Caesar promulgated a decree worded as follows:

---

[6] Wayne Blank, "Antiochus IV," *Daily Bible Study, accessed April 3, 2013, www.keyway.ca/htm2002/antoiv.htm.*

'Hyrcanus and his sons will preserve all their rights to the title of high priest, whether it was granted to them by law or by a free gift. If, subsequently a question arises concerning Jewish politics (polity), I desire that it be settle by referring to him.

All other measures notwithstanding, I allow their people [the Jews] to gather and organize their community following the customs of their fathers and according to their laws.'[7]

This favorable decree by Julius Caesar was approved after his death by the senate of the Roman Republic and later by Augustus Caesar. Jewish influence systematically grew and thrived throughout the Roman Empire. At the time of St. Paul, the Jewish population in Rome numbered tens-of thousands and was served by numerous synagogues.[8]

Some Roman Israelites were 'well-to-do . . .rich!' At that time, there were more than seventy gilded chairs in the leading synagogues around Alexandria. Only 'true wood artisans and gold metalsmiths' were commissioned to build these chairs. Many of these synagogues were among the most beautiful buildings in Jerusalem, Antioch, Syria and Alexandria.

The commerce in rice and other grains grown in Egypt and shipped to Rome was largely in the hands of Jewish merchants. The grain trade controlled by the Roman government made many Jewish merchants and seamen wealthy.

---

[7] Joseph M. Callewaert, *The World of St. Paul*, trans. *Michael J. Miller (San Francisco: Ignatius Press, 2011), pp. 13-21.*
[8] Ibid. *The World of St. Paul, p. 21*

There were Roman men who had themselves circumcised and practiced the Jewish religion and law. Even though these Romans followed the law handed down by Moses, many in the Roman 'cultivated' classes hated the Jews. *Cicero* described the Jewish religion as a *'barbarous superstition.'* *Juvenal,* a Roman poet of satire, ridiculed the 'Jews refusal to eat pork.' *Tacitus,* a senator and historian of the Roman Empire treated that "abominable race as sluggards because they did not work on the Sabbath day or during days of the Sabbatical year." *Seneca,* a 'philosopher, statesman, orator, and tragedian,'[9] wrote "This custom of that despised race is so widespread that it has been adopted in practice in all countries; the conquered have imposed their laws on the conquerors." In light of the ridicule, the Jewish historian *Flavius Josephus* retorted: "For a long time, there was great zeal among the masses for our religion; there is scarcely a Greek or barbarian city or nation in which the custom of resting on the seventh day is not observed."[10]

One might infer that the groundwork for the spread of Christianity looked promising. With Paul's new theology, he could address both Jews and Gentiles as he had command of both Hebrew and the Greek language. The Jewish Law was the *didaskolas* (teacher) that led the people to the Messiah, the Christ announced by the prophets of the Old Testament. It would now be the task of the disciples, the apostles, and St. Paul to proclaim Him, and spread the Gospel 'to the ends of the earth.'[11]

Rome continued to grow with, and without the Jews, and new conquered regions and peoples migrated to Rome; Rome became the meeting place for many diverse groups of people. Even the legionnaires, returning from wars and battles, returned to Rome rich and corrupted, now out of work and eager for pleasure.

---

[9] www.britannica.com/biography/Lucius-Annaeus-Senecus.

[10] William A. N. Whitson, *The Works of Josephus (Peabody, MA: Hendrickson Publishers, 1987), p 606.*

[11] Stanley, *Life Principles Bible, Acts 1:8.*

When a nation has arrived at the pinnacle of its power and is the mistress of the world, certain ambitions know no limit, and those with these ambitions place the nation's institutions at risk. If the nation does not find a *man or woman* who places the future of the homeland ahead of partisanship, there will be anarchy and tyranny. In our current calendar year 2020, we should digest, think about, and heed the wording of the above paragraph.

What happened next in the history of Rome is known by all:

- the relationship between Anthony and Cleopatra,

- the naval battle and victory of Octavius at Actium,

- the destruction of the republic,

- the accession to power of Octavius, who was proclaimed emperor under the name of Augustus.

The succession to the throne of Octavius was an important factor in the propagation of Christianity. All roads literally led to Rome, and those well paved highways, as well as the maritime trade routes, were rid of bandits and pirates. The Pax Romana, a relative peace, reigned throughout the world.

Chapter 1 Study Questions

1. Name five ways the Roman Empire helped spread the new Christian religion.

2. Why was *Kione* Greek important to the spread of Christianity?

3. Who were the Maccabees, and what did they accomplish?

4. How is *Hanukkah* tied to the Maccabees?

PAUL OF TARSUS

The city of Tarsus, on the Tarsus River, today is a city of sixty thousand inhabitants on the southeast coast of southern Anatolia, in modern-day Turkey. Its historical past was quite eventful. Over the course of the second millennium BC, Tarsus was the capital of the Hittite state of Kizzuwatna. In 698 BC it was captured by Sennacherib, King of Assyria.

Alexander the Great resided there in 333 BC. *Cicero*, a philosopher, trial lawyer, and one of the greatest orators of the Roman Empire in his capacity as governor of Roman Cilicia, resided in Tarsus in 50 BC. Julius Caesar visited the city in 47 BC.

In 41 BC Mark Antony lived there and rewarded the city for its resistance to Brutus and Cassius by exempting the citizens from all taxes. During the same year, Mark Antony invited Cleopatra, Queen of Egypt to visit Tarsus. Mark Anthony sought Cleopatra as an ally and later, she would become his lover.

The Queen's arrival was one of the most spectacular and pompous events in Greco-Roman history. "Her magnificent ship was filled with flowers and liberally sprinkled with exotic perfumes."[12] As she approached the city, winds blowing from the stern, perfumes and other scents in the air, those downwind could not only see her arrival but smell it as well. In the crowd assembled on the riverbanks, we might have found Paul's grandparents in the year 41 BC if his family ancestors lived there. Paul's parents and family were *Diaspora Jews*, living outside of Palestine.

Tarsus was a city rich in citizenry known for their love of science and arts. Many great thinkers, philosophers, teachers and counselors lived, or later moved on from Tarsus. Athenodorus Cananites, son of Sandon, a Stoic philosopher from the city of Canana close to Tarsus became a counselor of the emperor Augustus and tutor of Augustus's son, Claudius. There was a time when people in Ancient Rome stated, *"All teachers of thinking in Rome are from Tarsus."[13]*

The city of Tarsus was known for their superior textiles. Paul and his family worked in the textile industry as 'tentmakers.' Tents of that era were often made of cowhide or sheep skin and hair. The Jewish rabbinic writings recorded there was extensive commerce in textiles between Judea and Cilicia. Paul's family had good connection within the trade. They also supplied tents for the Roman Army.

Tarsus, and cities surrounding Tarsus had their rituals of paganism also. Every year in Scythia a city not far from Tarsus, the townspeople celebrated the Festival of Sacaea, the Syrian war goddess *Anaitis*, during the vernal equinox. It was a 'five-day *free-for all* affair highlighted by drunkenness, debauchery, and frenetic excesses.' [14]

---

[12]*'Cleopatra's Gate in Tarsus,' turkisharchaeonews.net/object/cleopatras-gate-tarsus, accessed Nov. 14, 2019.*

[13] Callewaert, *The World of St. Paul, p.23.*

[14] *"Anthenodorus Canaites," Encyclopaedia Britannica, last modified July 20, 1998, accessed April 3, 2017, www.britannica.com/biograph/Anthenodorus-Cananites.*

Against this backdrop, the most famous person from Tarsus was born, Saul of Tarsus, later known as *St. Paul the Apostle to the Gentiles.* He was born during the reign of Caesar Augustus between 5 BC and AD 5. He was circumcised on the eighth day and was named Sh'aul. Paul's name means 'desired'[15] in Hebrew, honoring the first king of Israel (Saul).[16] Sources of a 'particular Roman dialect' indicate that his surname also meant 'small.'[17]

Father Jerome, a fourth-century Christian writer, "knew a different possible history of Paul's birthplace. He wrote, Paul's parents "*were from Gischala in Galilee, A Jewish town twenty-five miles north of Sepphoris, saying that it was there Paul was born.*"[18] When the Jewish Revolts broke out after the death of Herod the Great in 4 BC, Jerome reports Paul and his parents were captured and as part of a large-scale exile of Galilean inhabitants from Palestine, were sent to Tarsus in Cilicia. If Jerome's account is valid, the parents of Paul, and the parents of Jesus, may have lived within miles of each other.[19]

Paul's family members *were Roman citizens*; "They had obtained Roman citizenship, possibly for loyal service to Rome, or perhaps by an accumulation of wealth and influence in their new province of Cilicia."[20] Paul was registered in the archives of one of the Roman *tribus* (tribes, a division of the state) in the capital far away on the

---

[15] Emphasis my own (Author's). The Greek-Hebrew word for *Sh'aul, Saul means desired and/or small*"; *In Paul's case it may be a safe assumption the name may have been in honor of King Saul.*

[16] James D. Tabor, *The Jesus Dynasty (Hammersmith, London: Simon & Schuster, and Harper Element, 2006), pg. 234.*

[17] Ibid. p. 234.

[18] "Sepphoris, the Great City of Lower Galilee," *Bible History Outline, accessed April 3, 2017. www.bible-History.com/sites/Sepphoris.html.*

[19] Father Jerome, *"Paul," in De Viris Illustribus, 646; Tabor, The Jesus Dynasty, p. 235.*

[20] Tabor, *The Jesus Dynasty, p. 235.*

banks of the Tiber River – Rome. Paul answered to two given names: *Sh'aul* among the Jews, and *Paulos* among the Gentiles.

Paul's father as a Roman citizen and man of prominence was ensured an imminent rank among his fellow citizens. Paul was a Roman citizen from birth, and when he became of age, he had the privilege of being sent to a school of Pharisees in Jerusalem. Luke in the Book of Acts states, "Paul's father was a Pharisee."[21]

Paul would enjoy the same privileges of citizenship when he became of age. "Citizenship in ancient Rome was a privileged political and legal status afforded to *free individuals'* with respect to Roman laws, property ownership, and governance."[22] Having the distinction of Roman citizenry was extremely important for Paul as we will see in his future.

Young Paul

Before Paul was able to speak, his parents taught him to 'touch a metal box on the doorpost that contained the *mezuzah,* a papyrus fragment inscribed with the *Shema: 'Hear O Israel, the Lord is our God, the Lord is One.*[23] *Shema* is the Hebrew word for *hear.*[24]

Later after learning his first words, his parents taught him to face distant Jerusalem, hands uplifted to heaven, repeating the *Shema,* a morning and evening prayer. Paul was to learn the text of a scriptural verse beginning and ending with the first and last letters of his Hebrew name.

---

[21] Stanley, *Life Principles Bible, Acts 23:6.*

[22] "Roman Citizenship," *Wikipedia, last modified January 25, 2017, accessed April 3, 2017, https//en.wikipedia.org/wiki/Roman_citizenship.*

[23] Stanley, *Life Principles Bible, Deuteronomy 6:4-6.*

[24] Ibid. "Life Lessons," Deuteronomy 6:4-6, p. 206.

Starting very young, Paul accompanied by his mother and father attended their synagogue where he sat with his mother behind the *mechitzah*; a partition that separated young Paul and his mother, along with other women and children, from the men. Upon returning home, Paul's mother and father would answer questions about what Paul had heard during the readings, or what may have stirred his curiosity. They would tell him stories of Abraham and Isaac, Jacob, Joseph and Moses. They certainly included the scriptures concerning King David, Queen Esther, and Daniel; they spoke of Judas Maccabeus who delivered the Jewish people from the tyrant Antiochus IV, and the restored Jewish Temple. They too, must have told Paul about the long-awaited messiah who would deliver Israel, and once and for all, restore the glorious kingdom of King David.

Though the father of the family was the prime factor in seeing his children would receive proper educations, Paul's mother was also very significant in his education. Paul at a young age was zealous in learning about his Jewish heritage. Paul's father helped further his education and started his possible interest in the *'trade of tentmaker'* (the trade may have been that of a leatherworker); St. Luke also writes in the Book of Acts Paul *was* a tentmaker.[25]

At, or close to the age of six, Paul was sent to a synagogue school, interestingly called a *'vineyard.'* Jewish parents believed their children, like a grapevine, needed to be "cleaned and pruned" so to produce fruit abundantly. The only disciplinary measures doled out at the vineyards were lashes with a leather strap. The classes were held in the open air. There were no blackboards, pencils, benches or desks. The students learned to read, write and count by forming letters or numbers in the sand; occasionally, they may have found a piece of pottery or scrap of papyrus to write on.

---

[25] Stanley, *Life Principles Bible Acts 18:3.*

The teachers recited the lessons out loud, repeating the main subjects over, and over, and over until the students had the lessons firmly implanted in their memories; repetition was the axiom for successful learning. The Jewish historian *Flavius Josephus* wrote in the first century AD: "From the age of reason, we learned the Law of Moses by heart, and it is, so to speak, anchored in our minds."[26]

At age thirteen, Paul was admitted as a "Son of the Law, or Son of the Commandment – *Bar Mitzvah* (Hebrew)." This is the time when a young Hebrew male is permitted to stand in front of his synagogue proudly proclaiming, "Today, I am a man."[27]

Paul's eventual trade as a tentmaker proved to be very useful over the course of his missionary journeys. Often, when he stayed in various regions or cities, Paul put his trade into practice and worked instead of relying on charity, handouts, or financial hospitality from others. He befriended two lifelong-friends and associates who were also tentmakers, *Priscilla and Aquila*, and worked with them in his trade in the city of Corinth.[28] Later Priscilla and Aquila accompanied Paul to Ephesus.

Very early in life, Paul began to 'practice what he preached;' "If anyone will not work, let him not eat."[29]

Chapter 2 Review Questions

1. What may have been the two greatest two exports from Tarsus? (Hints: College/University town; the manual trade of Paul)

2. What was a 'vineyard' regarding education in Paul's day?

3. Why was Roman citizenship a 'perk' in the times of Paul?

---

[26] Callewaert, *The World of Saint Paul, p.32.*

[27] Callewaert, *The World of Saint Paul. p.32.*

[28] Stanley, *Life Principles Bible, Acts 18:1-3.*

[29] Ibid. 2 Thessalonians 3:10.

PAUL THE PHARISEE

Paul was obviously a very inquisitive and intelligent man from the start, zealous for his Jewish heritage. When Paul was between the ages of fifteen and sixteen, his father sent him to Jerusalem to further his education in rabbinical studies in preparation to becoming a Pharisee. Paul's father was a Pharisee, and a man of means so he could send his son to Jerusalem.[30]

Schools of the Pharisees

In Jerusalem between AD 15 - and 30, two rabbinical schools existed; one founded by *Shammai*, the other by *Hillel*. Both were associated with the training of Pharisees, and stringently taught the Laws of Moses.[31]

Shammai was a Jewish scholar of the first century AD and an important personage in Judaism's *core work* of rabbinic literature, *the Mishnah*. He was the most eminent contemporary and the *halakhic*[32] opponent of Hillel and is invariably mentioned along

---

[30] Stanley, *Life Principles Bible, Acts 23:6.*

[31] Callewaert, *The World of St. Paul, p.39.*

[32] Halakha: *The Laws of Jewish Life/My Jewish Learning,* www.myjewishle-arning.com/article/halakhah-the, accessed November 15, 2019.

with Hillel.[33] *Halakha* is the collective body of Jewish religious laws derived from the written and oral *Torah*. It includes 613 *mitzvoth*, subsequent *Talmudic* rabbinic laws, and the customs and traditions compiled in the *Shulchan Aruch* (in English dubbed the Code of the Jewish Law).[34]

The other rabbinical school's founder was Hillel the Elder (ca. 110 BC – AD 10). Hillel, a famous Jewish leader was born in Babylon, and lived in Jerusalem during the time of King Herod. He is considered one of the most important personages in Judaic history, associated with the *Mishnah* and the *Talmud*. His lineage included a long line of rabbis, including Judah Ha-Nasi (credited with compiling the *Mishnah*), and Judah's son, Hillel the Younger.[35]

Paul enrolled in the school of Hillel, and the course study tended to follow the strict laws and traditions of Judaism and was directed by *Gamaliel* (nicknamed the *'Splendor of the Law'* as he commanded a thorough knowledge of the Torah, Jewish Law, Greek knowledge and language).[36] Gamaliel the Elder, or *Rabban* Gamaliel I, was a leading authority in the Sanhedrin in the early first century AD and was one of seven who merited the title of 'Rabban,' which was given to the most illustrious and intellectual doctors of the law. In one Christian tradition, Gamaliel was said to have converted to Christianity and is venerated as a saint along with his second son, Abibo. Jewish sources do not record a conversion to Christianity, but it is a possibility.

---

[33] 33 "Shammai," *Wikipedia, last modified March 23, 2017, accessed April 3, 2017, https//en.wikipedia.org/wiki/Shammai.*

[34] "Halakha," *Wikipedia, last modified December 31, 2015, accessed November 15, 2019, https://en.wikiquote.org/wiki/Halakha.*

[35] "Hillel the Elder," *Wikiquote, last modified January 3, 2017, accessed November 15, 2019, https://en.wikiquote.org/wiki/Hillel_the_Elder.*

[36] Callewaert, *The World of St. Paul, p.39.*

The Pharisees were one of three major sects of Judaism during the time of Christ. The other two were the Sadducees and the Essenes. Pharisees by far were the most influential and popular among the "everyday Jewish people, and were integrated into local communities while the Sadducees tended to be 'elite and aristocratic.'"[37]

The doctrines of the Pharisees included *predestination, the immortality of the soul, and a belief in spirit life* (teachings the Sadducees denied). They also believed in *a final reward for good works* and thought *the wicked were detained forever under the earth.* (The Jewish term, *Sheol* indicated an indifferent place of the dead and designated a special 'doom' in the afterlife of the wicked).[38]

Another belief of the Pharisees was *'the virtuous rose again and even migrated into other bodies.'* The Pharisees accepted the Old Testament scriptures and fostered the usual Jewish messianic hope which they gave a material and nationalistic twist.[39] It was inevitable in view of the Pharisees beliefs, they bitterly opposed Jesus and his teachings, and frequently, verbally clashing with him. Jesus's longest rebuke is found in the Book of Matthew, Chapter 23.[40]

The rise of the Jewish *scribes* closely associated with the Pharisees gave great impetus to Jewish legalism. The Pharisees somewhat of a quasi-fraternal order or religious society were the organized followers of the scribes in interpreting the scriptures; the Pharisees formalized the religion of the scribes and put it into practice.

---

[37] James D. Tabor, *The Jesus Dynasty (Hammersmith, London: Simon & Schuster and Harper Element, 2006) p. 105.*

[38] J.D. Douglas and Merrill C. Tenney, *NIV Compact Dictionary of the Bible (Grand Rapids, MI: Zondervan, 1989), p. 247.*

[39] Ibid. p.105.

[40] Stanley, *Life Principles Bible, Matthew 23 (all).*

Student Day, School of the Pharisees

The students in the school of Hillel would sit at the feet of their teaching rabbis. A passage or law was spoken from the Torah and then explained by what rabbis had said in the past. The students would debate and provide questions for the teaching rabbis and spoke among themselves. Day after day, week after week, month after month there were explanations, questions and answers, objections and final clarifications. Since the information and teachings were modeled on the same format, occasionally, it must have cause profound weariness, but this was how the rabbinic students studied and learned the Torah (the *Pentateuch*), the Prophets (*Nevi'im*), and the writings (*Kethuvim*).[41] *There was a tremendous amount of memory work.*

Archaeologists, historical experts, scholars, and researchers into the life of St. Paul believe and agree he had knowledge of the Jewish law so profound and intense he would have been considered a fanatical Pharisee and patriot (*a Zealot*). His ability to cite the law and scriptures verbatim indicated he was an ardent and accelerated student. Paul later wrote in Galatians, *"I advanced in Judaism beyond many of my contemporaries in my own nation, being more exceedingly zealous for the traditions of my fathers."*[42]

School of Greek Wisdom

Another important factor that played heavily into Paul's studies was Paul's close contacts with representatives and students in the *School of Greek Wisdom*. This was likely at the encouragement of Gamaliel. There was a Jewish proverb written, "Accursed be the one who eats pork, and accursed be the one who teaches the wisdom of the Greeks." Gamaliel denied that prejudice! He regularly visited a Greek philosopher whom he called 'friend and colleague.' Rabban

[41] Callewaert, *The World of St. Paul, p. 40.*

[42] Stanley, *Life Principles Bible, Galatians 1:13,14.*

Gamaliel was given permission to teach the students Greek due to his relationship with the Romans. Gamaliel's son, Rabbi Simeon even wrote, "There were a thousand pupils in my father's house; five hundred studied the Torah and five hundred studied Greek wisdom." Simeon's son, Rabbi Juda Ha-Nasi added, "Why speak Syriac in Palestine? Talk either Hebrew or Greek."[43]

Paul's association with the School of Greek Wisdom led to his further knowledge of and ability to read and speak the Greek language more fluently, not as one who had learned it laboriously late in life, but as a cultivated man who absorbed it from his earliest youth. It should be noted that growing up in Tarsus, Paul and the Jews were a minority living among a larger Greek population. He was exposed to and absorbed the Greek language early on.

Paul learned, and knew the Greek Bible extremely well, and cited scripture verbatim and consistently from the *Septuagint*, the Greek translation of the Old Testament. His use of Greek scripture was spoken and delivered in the natural dialect of a Greek. Just as Moses was an expert in the wisdom of the Egyptians, Paul drew upon the Greek wisdom handed down by the Hellenic culture.

At the conclusion of Paul's studies, and after his final examinations, he was seated among the rabbis. The ceremony included presenting him with a writing tablet covered by a thin film of wax signifying his 'duty to teach,' and Paul also received *a key* that symbolically *opened the treasures of knowledge and wisdom.* After the 'laying on of hands' (a gesture that signified the transmission of authority or office), *he received faculties and the right to be called by the title rabbi, or teacher.*

With studies completed, Paul returned to Tarsus where he began to teach the Jewish Law and words of the prophets. The enormous number of laws, 613 in the Torah alone, was a heavy

---

[43] "Gamaliel," *The Latter Rain Page, accessed April 3, 2017, www.latter-rain. com/train/gama.htm.*

burden for every Orthodox Jew (Paul did not forget this later after his Damascus road conversion when he turned his focus towards the Gentiles). In future scripture, Paul did not impose what he considered now *burdensome* Jewish Law and tradition on the Gentiles. Also, upon his return to Tarsus, Paul worked closely with his father and continued to learn the trade of a 'master tentmaker.'[44]

Even though Pharisees were generally lambasted in the New Testament, there were Pharisees during the early Christian movement of renown: Nicodemus (John 3:1,2), Gamaliel (Acts 5:34,35), and of course St. Paul of Tarsus.[45] Many Pharisees over the course of Jesus's life were very sympathetic to, and believed in '*the Word*' and the theology of Christianity.[46]

Another Pharisee who lived after the life of Christ was *Flavius Josephus* (AD 37-ca.- 100). Josephus authored what has become, for Christianity perhaps, the most significant extrabiblical writings of the first century. His works are the principal source for the history of the Jews from the reign of Antiochus Epiphanes (175-163 BC) to the fall of Masada in AD 73 (the final events of the First Jewish-Roman War occurring between AD 73 -to AD 74 on and around a large hilltop in current-day Israel[47]). Therefore, his works are incomparable in value for determining the setting of late intertestamental and New Testament times.[48]

Could Paul and Josephus Flavius have ever met? Those chances are very unlikely, but it can be said both men contributed

---

[44] Callewaert, *The Life of St. Paul, p. 33.*

[45] Douglas and Tenney, *NIV Compact Dictionary, p. 454.*

[46] James D. Tabor, *The Jesus Dynasty, p. 107.*

[47] Siege of Masada-*Wikipedia/en.Wikipedia.org/Siege_of_Masada. Accessed November 17, 2019.*

[48] William A.M. Whiston (trans.) *The Works of Josephus (Peabody, MA: Hendrickson Publishers, 2010) p. ix.*

tremendously to the history of the times and the Jewish nation of Israel.

Chapter 3 Study Questions

1. What were the *three primary doctrines* of the Pharisees living in Israel?

2. Who was Gamaliel? What was a nickname, or honorary name bestowed on him during Paul's day? Why?

3. How did the School of Greek Wisdom benefit Paul, and his future?

4. What is *Kione* Greek

THE DAMASCUS ROAD

Paul the Zealot Pharisee

From scripture, we know Paul before his conversion was a zealous persecutor and prosecutor of Christian Jews and followers of *the Way*.' The following statements are in Paul's own words:

1. "I was violently persecuting the church of God and was trying to destroy it."[49]

2. "As to zeal, a persecutor of the Church . . . ."[50]

3. "I am the least of the apostles, unfit to be called an apostle because I persecuted the church of God."[51]

4. "Being zealous for God . . . I persecuted *the Way*' up to the point of death or binding both men and women and putting them in prison."[52]

---

[49] Stanley, *Life Principles Bible, Galatians 1:13,14.*
[50] Ibid. Philippians 3:6.
[51] Ibid. 1 Corinthians 15:9
[52] Ibid. Acts 22:3,4.

Both Paul and Luke use the term zealous,[53] which in Jewish religious context often denotes *paralegal and possibly lethal action* against those considered apostates.[54] When Paul found pockets of '*the Way*,' the title given to the new movement of Jesus Christ, he publicly humiliated them and forced people from their homes (men, women and children). He dealt with apostates harshly, including beatings, whippings, or possibly *'stoning to death.'* Paul's reputation as a *Zealot* to the highest degree proceeded him wherever he went. If it were possible that Paul may be knocking at one's door, those inside would be wise to use a restraint, or run.

Paul saw his mission as a Pharisee to *uphold and zealously maintain the tenets of the Jewish Law.* If it meant the death penalty, then Paul standing his ground subjected apostates to the death penalty. *In the New Perspective on Paul,* James D. G. Dunn points out the three striking features of zeal thus understood by Paul and the Pharisees in the early days of Christianity:

- First, in each case, *zeal was an unconditional commitment to maintain Israel's distinctiveness,* to prevent the purity of its *covenant set-apartness to God* from being adulterated or defiled, and to defend its religious and national boundaries.

- Second, *a Zealot was ready to do this by force*; in each case it is the thorough going commitment expressed precisely in the slaughtering of those who threatened Israel's distinctive covenant status that merited the description of "zeal" or "zealot."

- Third, *this zeal was directed* not only at Gentiles who threatened Israel's boundaries but also against fellow Jews.[55]

---

[53] Ibid. Acts 22:4

[54] Callewaert, *The World of St. Paul, p.44.*

[55] James D.G. Dunn, *The New Perspective on Paul, p. 361.*

The followers of '*the Way*' had been taught a new belief movement and system from the teachings of the rabbi Jesus Christ. Instead of following the tenets of the Torah, the new Messiah taught that *reconciliation with God led to the grace of God.* After grace, *comes justification, sanctification, salvation, and ultimately "eternal life in Heaven."*[56] The rabbi in the person of Jesus Christ led the followers to believe there was an alternative, new 'way to salvation and eternal life,' versus the Jewish Laws handed down by Abraham and Moses.

What Angered the Pharisees in Paul's Time (Brief History of the Pharisees)

The religious belief system incorporated by the Pharisees began its rise between 175 BC and 164 BC. This time coincides with Antiochus IV Epiphanes attempt to Hellenize and assimilate the Jewish population in Jerusalem. The Pharisees were the sect that organized the Jews and helped them organize their national religious consciousness and identity. Pharisaism (the doctrines and practices of the Pharisees, or a *hypo*-observance of the letter of religious or moral law without regard for the spirit) became more formalized during the reign of John Hyrcanus (175 – 104 BC). Hyrcanus I(175 BC -to 104 BC) was a high priest and ruler of the Jewish nation from 135 BC – to 104 BC. Under his reign, the Hasmonean Kingdom of Judea in ancient Palestine attained power and great prosperity. Pharisees with popular backing, and the Sadducees, a more aristocratic and elitist sect that comprised the priesthood, became well-defined.[57]

Paul and his fellow Pharisees were the religious leaders of the Jews, strictly abiding by the Torah, and intently opposed to any secularization of Judaism by the pagan '*Greek thought*' that

[56] Irving L. Brittle Jr, *It's Not Rocket Science–The Theology of St. Paul the Apostle (Pen House Publishing, Sheridan, WY, 2020) p. 35.*

[57] "John Hyrcanus I," *Encyclopaedia Brittannica, last updated July 20, 1998, accessed April 3, 2017,* www.britannia.com/biography/John-Hyrcanus-I.

penetrated Jewish life after the Alexandrian conquest.[58] Obviously to Paul, '*the Way*' was a new movement in conflict with the Torah and the tenets of Jewish Law. It would not be tolerated and was considered a high form of blasphemy. But, Paul after his conversion "became the major proponent of inclusion of Gentile believers versus prosecuting and persecuting those same believers." Even though Paul transformed his basic beliefs, he was *never* an anti-Semite.

'To the Jews I became as a Jew in order to win Jews; to those under the Torah, I became as one under the Torah – though not actually being under the Torah – that I might win those under the Torah; to those outside the Torah (Gentiles), I became as one outside the Torah, not being without the law, but under the *Torah of Christ* – that I might win those outside the Torah.'[59]

No longer did Gentiles who desired to be part of the *people of God* believe they had to convert to Judaism. The Gentiles were essentially released from the meal requirements and limits on their foods and drinks. Circumcision, a sure sign of a Jewish male was something Paul abandoned as did many of his associates. After Paul's conversion to 'Christology,' and his eventual title St. Paul, Apostle to the Gentiles, the requirement of circumcision was *a Jewish Law* he did drop. His new view on circumcision, among others, caused many of his fellow Jews to question *his* Judaism.

Circumcision was *vigorously* debated between Paul and the original apostles, especially St. Peter.[60] Paul came to believe circumcision was an *act of the flesh* following Jewish Law, and believed that 'true grace is a free gift from God and doesn't have to be earned by doing good works or proving yourself as a Jew by

---

[58] Douglas and Tenney, *Compact Dictionary of the Bible, pp.453-454.*

[59] Stanley, *Life Principles Bible, 1 Corinthians 9:20,21.*

[60] Stanley, *Life Principles Bible, Acts 21:21.*

being circumcised.' Circumcision was not high on Paul's priority list that evidenced one's faith in God.[61]

Messianic Judaism

In modern vernacular, Paul had become a Messianic Jew. Messianic Judaism is a movement that combines Christianity, importantly, the Christian belief that Jesus was the messiah with elements of Judaism and Jewish tradition. "This Nazarene movement, led by James, Peter, and John, was by any historical definition a messianic movement within Judaism.[62]

> 'No one in the Jesus movement was thinking about a *new religion* but rather a restoration and fulfillment of the promises that God had made with Israel through its leaders and prophets. This included the promise of the *new covenant* that Jeremiah had predicted, but it was a *renewed covenant* with the house of Israel and the house of Judah,' as the prophet Jeremiah had stated, and as Jesus had expected in choosing the twelve apostles, one to rule each of the twelve tribes of a *"regathered Israel."*[63] [64]

> 'The most unsettling aspect of Paul's new and *possibly mystical gospel* for members of the messianic movement that John the Baptist and Jesus had inaugurated was his view of the *temporary nature* of the Torah and/or Jewish Law, and a "spiritual" redefinition of who constituted the people of Israel. Judaism in the Roman world was diverse, but in all its forms there were two common elements: the central place of the Torah and God, and

---

[61] Ibid. Acts 15:5-11.

[62] James D. Tabor, *The Jesus Dynasty, pp. 239, 240.*

[63] Stanley, *Life Principles Bible, Jeremiah 31:3.*

[64] Tabor, p.240.

the belief that the people of Israel were God's chosen nation.' [65]

Christ had commanded the twelve apostles, and disciples to preach the *"Good News and New Way,"*[66] as it was known in the time after his crucifixion and resurrection. There was a very large contingency of Christian Jews in – and around Jerusalem. Shortly after Christ's crucifixion, the apostles were thrown into prison, and the Sanhedrin had plans to execute them. *Gamaliel* intervened advocating for their release according to the rulings of the seventy-one members of the Sanhedrin. As a result, the apostles were spared and released.[67]

Disciples of Christ continued to grow and then elected seven deacons (*diakonos, Greek for* 'servant') to assist in caring for the poor and administering the material goods from what they already were beginning to call the church (*ekklesia*). *Stephen* filled with the Holy Spirit was one of the deacons.

Stephen preached the 'good news' in the synagogues as the numbers grew due to the migration of Jews from throughout the diaspora back to Jerusalem. The Pharisees debated furiously with Stephen and never seemed to have the last word; this exacerbated their hatred of Stephen. Stephen was subsequently arrested, brought before the Sanhedrin, tried, condemned to death, driven from the city, and stoned to death. Paul was part of the contingency and consented to the murder. Paul's status as rabbi did not prevent him from participating actively in the stoning of Stephen, but he was "content to watch over the murderer's garments.'[68] [69] As for

---

[65] Tabor, *The Jesus Dynasty, p. 239.*

[66] Tabor, *The Jesus Dynasty, p.45.*

[67] Stanley, *Life Principles Bible Acts 5:34-39.*

[68] Ibid. Acts 7:58.

[69] Ibid. Acts 22:20.

Stephen, whose name in Greek means 'crown,' he became the first martyr of the Christian Church.

Even after this barbarous act to Stephen, Paul was compared to a 'wild boar in a prolific vegetable garden determined to destroy everything in its path.' Paul *laid waste to the Church of the Way'* dragging men and women from their homes, binding and incarcerating them in prisons known for their horrible interior conditions.[70] If there were a *silver lining* to all the arrests and incarcerations, it gave good reason for the disciples to disperse throughout the country and continue to spread the gospel.[71] Many of the new believers fled to Damascus.

After Paul purged Jerusalem of the followers of '*the Way,*' he set his sights on Damascus. "Still breathing threats and murder against the disciples of Jesus,"[72] his next stop would be Damascus and the synagogues in the city approximately 150 miles north. Paul knew the road well as it was a highway that would eventually lead him back home to Tarsus.

Damascus

Over time the city of Damascus was referred to as *The Eye of the Desert* or *The Pearl of the Orient.* Damascus lays claim to being one of the oldest continually inhabited cities in the world. The city has a long history of personages from the Bible:

---

[70] Ibid. Acts 8:3, 22:4.

[71] Ibid. Acts 8:4,5

[72] Ibid.Acts 9:1.

- It is mentioned in the Biblical story of Abraham,[73] who indeed is said in later (Hellenistic) tradition to have reigned in Damascus,[74]

- Eliezer, known as a faithful servant of Abraham,

- King David stationed a garrison that subsequently opposed Solomon's plans.

- Ananias helped Paul with his conversion and regain his eyesight after the Damascus road event and encounter with Jesus Christ.

Damascus was subject successively to Assyrian, Babylonian, Persian, and Greco-Macedonian empire rule. Damascus plays a part in Muslim eschatological tradition as the place where Jesus will descend to destroy the Antichrist; this may have figured in a branch of Christian tradition from which the Muslims took over the expectation.[75]

The plums of Damascus were delicious and famous, along with its damask linen and damascened swords. These swords were made with Damascus steel, a type of alloy used for manufacturing blades in the Near East – wootz steel, imported from southern India. The swords were characterized by distinctive patterns of banding and mottling reminiscent of flowing water. Such blades were reputed

---

[73] Stanley, *Life Principles Bible, Genesis 14:15, 15:2*

[74] F. F. Bruce, *Paul: Apostle of the Heart Set Free (Grand Rapids, MI: William B. Eerdmans Publishing Company, 1997), 76.*

[75] Ibid. p. 77.

to be tough, resistant to shattering, and capable of being honed to a sharp, resilient edge.[76] [77]

Change in Destiny on the Damascus Road

As Paul approached the city, his whole world, his life as he had lived it – *everything* changed in the *blink of an eye and a "flash of light."*[78] The following is in Paul's own words:

> 'At midday, O king, I saw in the way a light from heaven above the brightness of the sun, shining around about me and them which journeyed with me. And when we were all fallen to earth, I heard a voice speaking to me, and saying in Hebrew tongue,
>
> "Saul, Saul, why are you persecuting me? It is hard to kick against the goads."
>
> And Paul said, "Who are You, Lord?"
>
> And He said, "I am Jesus whom you are persecuting."[79]
>
> Jesus added, "Get up! Go into Damascus and there you will be told of all that will be **appointed** to you to do."[80]

---

[76] "Damascus Steel," *Wikipedia, last modified March 21, 2017, accessed April 3, 2017, http://Wikipedia.org/wiki/Damascus_steel.*

[77] Today, Christians living in Damascus have been summarily uprooted and forced to migrate. Their churches have been destroyed, and unfortunately many Christians have been brutally "executed and tortured" at the hands of Islamic extremists. Damascus, today, is in ruins.

[78] Stanley, *Life Principles Bible, Acts 9:3.*

[79] Ibid. Acts 26:13-15.

[80] Ibid. Acts 22:10.

Obviously this magnificent, God sent occurrence would have been a life-changing experience for any man or women. In our modern colloquialism, Paul was commanded to make a *'major career change.'*

The blinding light and apparition of Jesus Christ on the Damascus road had rendered Paul temporarily blind. Although his eyes were open, he saw nothing and had to be led into Damascus, and after arriving, "he neither ate nor drank for three days."[81] Paul was welcomed into the home of a man named *Judas on Straight Street*. Also living in Damascus was a disciple of renown by the name of *Ananias*, to whom the Lord spoke directly. One can only imagine what Ananias must have felt when asked by the Lord to meet the renowned Pharisee known as Saul, *the Zealot Pharisee*.

> "But the Lord said to Ananias, 'Get up and go to the street called Straight, and inquire at the house of Judas for a man from Tarsus named Saul, for he is praying and he has seen in *a vision* of a man named Ananias come in and lay his hands on him, so that he might regain his sight.'"

> But Ananias answered, "Lord, I have heard from many about this man, how much harm he did to Your saints at Jerusalem; and here he has authority from the chief priests to bind all who call on Your name."

> But the Lord said to him, "Go, for he is a *'chosen instrument of Mine,'* to bear My name before the Gentiles and kings and the sons of Israel; for I will show him how much he must suffer for My name's sake."[82]

Of course, Ananias obeyed the Lord.

---

[81] Ibid. Acts 9:9.

[82] Stanley, *Life Principles Bible, Acts 9:11-16.*

He entered the home of Judas, laid his hands on Saul, and said to him, "Brother Saul, the Lord Jesus, who appeared to you on the road by which you were coming, has sent me so that you may regain your sight and be filled with the Holy Spirit. And immediately there fell from his eyes something like scales, and he regained his sight, got up, was baptized, and took food and was strengthened.[83] Now for several days he was with the disciples who were at Damascus."[84]

Paul spent days, maybe weeks, with the disciples in Damascus, beginning without delay to preach in the synagogues, proclaiming, "Jesus is the Son of God – the messiah promised by the prophets."[85] All hearing him continued to be amazed, and said, "Is not this he who destroyed those who called on His name in Jerusalem, and who had come here for the purpose of bringing them bound before the chief priests?"[86]

Paul's Conversion

One can only imagine what those who met and listened to Paul thought and felt. Obviously, something very dramatic, possibly surreal, had occurred over a short period of time to Paul. Biblical scholars still debate if Paul saw an apparition of Christ; this debate is fueled by St. Luke in the book of Acts as he makes no mention of Paul's seeing Christ. In scripture St. Luke claims Paul *did not* see Christ but only heard His voice. Paul in his version says *he did see Christ*. Either way, this would have been an extremely powerful encounter for anyone, and the *"voice"* addressed Paul *"personally,"* and most certainly caught his attention.

---

[83] Ibid. Act 9:17-19.

[84] Ibid. Acts 9:20.

[85] Ibid. Acts 9:20.

[86] Ibid. Acts 9:21.

From Paul's Damascus road experience of seeing and hearing Christ, he knew *he had been chosen* by God to spread the Gospel. Paul began to believe in his *heart and mind* he was an equal apostle to the original twelve. "Paul began to develop his views of *Christology* based on his *mystical experiences* while spending three years in the Arabian desert and Damascus but would also draw upon a complex set of speculative Jewish traditions as well."[87] Up to this point, Paul's ideas of how to find salvation in and to be "right before the Lord" were based on Jewish Law and traditions (good works). From now on, an acceptance and belief in Jesus Christ as the Messiah and Son of God would fulfill the requirements of salvation and eternal life – especially important for the future Gentiles he ministered, and Jews.

There is no evidence Paul ever met or heard Jesus teach while the latter was alive in human form. If he had witnessed the events surrounding Jesus's crucifixion during the Passover in A D 30, he never mentioned it. His connection to Jesus was based on his own *visionary experiences* in which he claimed to have "*seen*" Jesus shortly after his crucifixion.[88]

"Paul believed his calling had been foreordained: 'He set me apart before I was born and called me through His grace . . . that I might preach Him among the Gentiles.[89] [90] "He also claimed to hear a 'disembodied voice' he identified as 'words of Jesus.'"[91] [92]

It can be called one of the greatest transformations of mind and spirit in Biblical history took place on the Damascus road. Saul,

---

[87] Tabor, *The Jesus Dynasty, p. 239.*

[88] Stanley, *Life Principles Bible, 1 Corinthians 9:1,2; 15:6–8.*

[89] Ibid. Galatians 1:15,16

[90] Tabor, The Jesus Dynasty, p. 237.

[91] Stanley, *Life Principles Bible, 2 Corinthians 12:9; 1 Thessalonians 4:15; 1 Corinthians 11:23;*

[92] Tabor, p.237.

later to be known better as Paul would be the "chosen instrument of Mine (God, Jesus Christ)"[93] who would minister, spread the Gospel of Jesus Christ to Jews and Gentiles alike, and place the movement and theology of Christianity, '*the Way,*' in hearts, minds and souls of new believers in the Roman Empire and over time, the world.

Three Years in the Arabian Desert and Damascus

According to Biblical history and Paul's own words in scripture, he did not stay in Damascus for an extended length of time. We know he left Damascus and went to Arabia. This rather extraordinary decision to travel to the Arabian Desert(s) is not recorded or mentioned in the Book of Acts. St. Luke claimed that Paul traveled to Jerusalem after his Damascus road experience, and even met the apostles. Paul swore that was not the case.[94] Either St. Luke knew nothing about the Arabian sojourn, or he was so keenly interested in having Paul linked with the Jerusalem apostles that he may have purposely ignored it. St. Luke was not present in Damascus when Paul had his Damascus Road experience.

So why would Paul have gone to Arabia, and what were the Biblical boundaries of Arabia? *Strabo*, a Greek geographer and historian whose '*Geography*' is the only extant work covering the entire range of peoples and countries known to both Greeks and Romans during the reign of Augustus (27 BC – AD 16), and its numerous quotations from technical literature, provide a remarkable account of the state of Greek geographical science, as well as the history of the countries it surveyed.[95]

Strabo explained that Arabia Felix included the entire Arabian Peninsula bound by the Red Sea and the Persian Gulf. But what

---

[93] Stanley, *Life Principles Bible, Acts 9:15.*

[94] Ibid. Galatians 1:17,18.

[95]"Strabo," *Encyclopaedia Britannica, last modified August 9, 2012, accessed April 3, 2017, www.britannica.com/biography/Strabo.*

would Arabia have suggested, or offered to a Jew who lived in the first century in Judea or Damascus? The first-century Jewish historian *Josephus* provides one answer:

> 'Arabia could be seen to the east from a tower in Jerusalem. More specifically, it was contiguous to Herodian territory running along the southern border of the Roman province of Syria. Petra was the royal seat of Arabia, hence the name Arabia Petra, or Arabia belonging to Petras.

> The mountainous encircled city however was the capital and central city of the Nabateans, hence another name, Arabia of the Nabateans.'

This and other geographical markers clearly indicate when Paul mentioned going to 'Arabia,' he meant the Nabatean territory, modern day Jordan. Paul's on- and off excursions to Jordan occurred between 30 AD and 33 AD (close proximity with the crucifixion and resurrection of Jesus Christ).[96] It was neither by accident nor arbitrary choice that Paul decided to go to Arabia immediately after his initial vision (encounter) with the spirit of Christ. A common thread is he went to reflect on his *new directive* from Christ, perhaps to commune with God in the vicinity of *'Horeb, the mountain of God'* where Moses and Elijah had communed with Him in days past. This may have been part of the purpose 'for going away,' but *his three-day blindness* in Damascus had been more than adequate for him to seek a re-orientation of the mind.[97]

Paul certainly sought periods of isolation, perhaps in the mountains, caves, or open desert praying, meditating and

---

[96] "Jerome-Murphy-O'Conner, "What Was Paul Doing in Arabia?" October,1994, accessed April 3, 2017, *Biblical Archaeology Society (BAS Library), review 10.5.*

[97] F. F. Bruce, *Paul: The Heart of an Apostle Set Free, p.81.*

attempting to sort through his dramatic visions and experiences. Paul traveled to desolate areas not to confer with any human, but to hear directly from Jesus Christ: "For I would have you know brethren, that the Gospel which was preached by me is no man's gospel. For I did not receive it of man, neither was I taught it, but by the revelation of Jesus Christ." [98]

"One particular ascent experience was one of *many visions* and revelations Paul received. His noted experience was so extraordinary that he believed there was danger that he would fall victim to pride knowing he among all human beings had been allowed to see and hear such forbidden mysteries. Consequently, Christ allowed a messenger of Satan to harass Paul with a physical affliction:[99]

> 'Because of the surpassing greatness of the revelations, for this reason, to keep me from exalting myself, there was given me a thorn in the flesh, a messenger from Satan to torment me – to keep me from exalting myself. Concerning this I implored the Lord three times that it might leave me. And He has said to me, "My grace is sufficient for you, for power is perfected in weakness." Most gladly, therefore, I will rather boast about my weaknesses, so that the power of Christ may dwell in me. Therefore, I am well content with weakness, with insults, with distresses, with persecutions, with difficulties, for Christ's sake; for when I am weak, then I am strong.'[100]

In a sense like the original twelve apostles Paul had his own personal, private three years with Jesus Christ who now was "the glorified heavenly cosmic and spiritual Christ." Paul later taught,

[98] Stanley, *Life Principles Bible, Galatians 1:11-13.*

[99] A. N. Wilson, *Paul: The Mind of the Apostle (New York: W.W. Norton, 1998)* *p.75.*

[100] Stanley, *Life Principles Bible, 2 Corinthians 12:7-10.*

"Jesus was a divine preexistent heavenly being, created as the 'firstborn' of all God's creation. He existed in the "form of God and was equal to God."[101] [102]

Paul's conversion was not a 'sudden one day event' as maybe put forth in the Book of Acts. Paul called his revelation in Jesus Christ as *spiritually taught* implying 'periods of heavenly tutoring that would involve "*visions and revelations of the Lord*."' Paul never specifies 'exactly' how long he spent in Arabia, but does note it was "*three years* after his *vision of Christ* on the Damascus road" he did go to Jerusalem to meet the apostles Peter and James (the brother of Jesus, a.k.a. James the Just).[103]

Paul's first visit to Jerusalem after the Damascus road revelation apparently was clandestine, only meeting Peter and James. *Barnabas*, a lifelong close friend and associate of Paul likely arranged the meeting as there was still suspicion as to the character of Paul and possible motives for wanting to meet the apostles. Paul wanted to '*tell his personal story*' and convey his own experiences of seeing, meeting and reveling in the Holy Spirit, and to gain a measure of acceptance from the original apostles.[104] From scripture, Paul "abided with him (Peter) for fifteen days"[105]

Chapter 4 Study Questions

1. What was Paul's reputation as a Pharisee? Why were new believers of *the Way* afraid of Paul?

2. What prompted Paul to make a trip to Damascus, and what was his mission?

3. Who was Ananias? How did he help Paul?

---

[101] Ibid. *John 8:18,19, 10:36, 14:6.*

[102] Dunn, *The Theology of Paul the Apostle, p.40.*

[103] Stanley, *Life Principles Bible*, **Galatians 1:18.19.**

[104] Ibid. Galatians 1:18.

[105] Ibid. Galatians 1:18.

4. Why may the Lord have left Paul temporarily blinded after his immediate Damascus road experience?

5. How did Arabia (modern day Jordan) play a role in Paul's life? How long did Paul stay in Damascus and Arabia?

Chapter 5

DECADENCE OF PAGAN RELIGIONS

Paul worked in his home area in Antioch, Syria and Cilicia after his return from Jerusalem and meeting Peter and James, but we have no detailed information after that. Over a period of eleven years (AD 36-to AD 47), and three years after his Damascus road event, Paul lived and worked in his home area. This time lapse is referred to as the 'intermediate years,' and Paul being a pastor, evangelist, and missionary likely helped new believers and start new churches.[106]

Paul surely encountered people in his missionary work who were pagan. He also would confront *Judaizers* who challenged his new theology as they did in Jerusalem and every-city he visited on his future three (possibly six) missions.

For millennia, people around the Mediterranean populated the invisible realm with a multitude of gods and goddesses in human form who were distinguished from mere mortals only by their perceived powers and immortality. The Greeks based their religion on the poems of *Homer, even Hesiod,* and they were considered

---

[106] Risto Santala, PAUL'S INTERMEDIATE YEARS, www.ristosantala. com/rsla/Paul/paul08.html, November 17, 2019, accessed November 21, 2019.

quasi-sacred. These were gods of arbitrary pleasure with no morality. The traits associated with these gods included greed, sensuality, and jealous thievery; most were vindictive scoundrels. Stories about Greek gods did nothing 'to lift the heart or calm the anxiety of mysteries.' They did not inspire the worshippers with a desire to be good, or moral.

The ancients were content to offer purely formalistic worship to the hidden entities that 'moved the world,' provided the ceremonies were conducted with the prescribed pomp and pageantry. The pagan religions were protected or supported by local ruling classes that decided which gods should be venerated and to whom sacrifices could be offered.

The Greek gods of the Roman's official religion numbered twelve: Jupiter (Zeus) the king; Juno, the wife of Jupiter; Minerva goddess of wisdom; Vulcan and Vesta, respectively the gods of fire; Ceres, goddess of the harvest; Neptune, god of the sea; Venus, goddess of love and beauty; Mars, god of war; Mercury, god of eloquence and commerce; Apollo, goddess of poetry and music; and finally, Diana, goddess of festivals and hunting.

When Paul arrived in Athens during his second missionary journey and while waiting for his associates to join him, he had ample time to look-around and notice a city inundated with idols and statues. One of Paul's truest 'pet-peeves' was the coveting of idols and idol worship. But there was 'one altar' with the inscription: *"TO AN UNKNOWN GOD;"* Paul had the perfect segue to inform the Athenians:

'Therefore, what you worship in ignorance, this I
proclaim to you. "The God who made the world and
all things in it, since He is Lord of heaven and earth,
does not dwell in temples made with hands."' [107]

---

[107] Stanley, *Life Principles Bible, Acts 17:23-26.*

The idea of true religious piety was foreign (as we may know and view it today) to the minds and souls of many people living in the Roman Empire. Nothing remained but empty idolatrous cults, superstitious rituals, and magic; none of which satisfied the desire for an assurance of happiness. Pessimism reigned! Uneasiness therefore tormented souls. But there were men and women who did seek salvation in the new spiritual movement called '*the Way*' centered in Jesus Christ.

There were many leaders during this era who came-and left with the title of 'savior,' which was given to many ancient and newer divinities and rulers who desired to be shielded from the threats of life and death. Other religions in which Greeks and Romans participated were the 'mystery religions' associated with Oriental cults including 'Attis and Cybele in Asia Minor and Osiris and Isis in Egypt.'

Issues the Greek and Romans religions scarcely touched on included *the concept of sin and the idea of purity of soul*. They did somewhat understand purity regarding bathing and fasting, but the idea of *inner moral purity* (purity of the soul) was foreign.

'The beginning of the Christian era was a great age of spiritual awakening, a quest for truth, and a search for the One True God. One God-seeker, one of the greatest among all next to Jesus Christ was Paul of Tarsus. "He was the instrument chosen" by the One True God to preach and spread the universal religion in a common language throughout an empire under the aegis of Rome.'[108]

---

[108] Callewaert, *The World of St. Paul, p. 72.*

Chapter 6

PAUL'S FIRST MISSION
THE SPREAD OF CHRISTIANITY

The second half of the Book of Acts focuses on two primary features that are in contrast with opening nine chapters:

1. St. Luke presents the missionary journeys and ministry of Paul in a broad sweep and documents Paul's work in Cyprus, Galatia, Thessalonica, Athens, Corinth, Ephesus and many cities and territories to which he traveled.

2. St. Luke pays close attention to 'the ripple effect' of the Gospel in large cities of the Gentile world; finally, in the city of Rome. St. Luke befriended Paul in a heartfelt manor, accompanied him on missions, encouraged his ministry and the spread of the Gospel.

St. Luke explains how Paul expanded his ministry of preaching and establishing (planting) new Christian churches during the three missions but is silent in regarding Paul's whereabouts and life after he reached Rome and said nothing of 'The Collection' or Paul's martyrdom.

42

Paul's first missionary journey started in 47 – 49 (50) AD, and the beginning of the mission initially left from the church in Antioch, Syria considered by many to be Paul's 'home church.' The church was located close to Damascus, Jerusalem, and on the route to his home in Tarsus and Cilicia. A large contingency of Gentiles lived within the region as well as Jews who escaped the initial purging of the churches of *'the Way'* in Jerusalem by the Pharisees - and Paul.

Leaders in the Antioch church came from multiethnic roots, but all tended to possess a remarkable sensitivity to divine leadership. The church 'elders' set aside special periods of time to concentrate on receiving divine leadership from their congregational members, and as the believers sought divine guidance, they learned God was calling three of their outstanding leaders for a special task.[109] The pre-departure of Paul, Barnabas and John Mark was accompanied by congregational prayer and fasting. The 'laying on of hands,' neither a formal ordination nor a commission to apostolic office, was an act of blessing where the church expressed its unity in supporting the ministry of Paul, Barnabas and John Mark.

Barnabas accompanied Paul throughout his first missionary journey. It should also be noted Barnabas was the acting intermediary in Jerusalem introducing Paul to Peter and James after his three years in Arabia and Damascus. John Mark, Barnabas's cousin, served as co-worker for a portion of the first mission. John Mark would be the author of the *Gospel of Mark*.

Paul and Barnabas never stayed long in any one location during the first mission as Paul's *'appointment'* was to spread the Gospel to as many potential believers as possible. Paul's 'adopted policy and modus operandi' involved entering a city, finding a synagogue, establishing a Christian foundation among residents (and local officials) who responded to his message of Christ and moving

---

[109] Stanley, *Life Principles Bible, Acts 13: 2,3.*

on to another city often under pressure 'to move on' from local authorities, or possible signs of 'divine direction.'   Paul focused his ministry initially in the synagogues where he found Jews and proselytes who accepted the Old Testament scriptures and had a *basic* understanding by what he meant when referring to '*Jesus Christ as the long-awaited messiah.*'

Where the synagogues were populated with Jews who understood the teachings of the Old Testament, often there was a large contingency of non-Jews (Gentiles) who wanted to listen to Paul's message; non-Jews were not welcomed within the synagogues and often non-Jews would hear his messages at the home of one of Paul's disciples or 'town squares' where no restrictions prevented anyone from hearing the Gospel.

From his first penetration into Gentile populated communities in Antioch, Paul, Barnabas, and Mark sailed east to the island of Cyprus before traveling to the mainland of Asia Minor and visiting the cities of Perga, Pisidian Antioch, Iconium, Lystra and Derbe, all in the region of Lycaonia. After landing on Cyprus, he moved inland to the greater populated 'political' centers. The first city visited was the eastern city of Salamis and from there, on to the island's seat of government, Paphos.

In Paphos Paul encountered and was opposed by a Jewish magician and false Jewish prophet named Bar-Jesus (Hebrew for 'son of Joshua'), or Elymas (Elymas was the term designating this man as a magician). Elymas opposed Paul's preaching as he saw it a 'threat to his own livelihood.' Paul met his opposition with strong action and brought "judicial blindness on Elymas." The Roman proconsul Sergius Paulus, a "man of intellect" was overwhelmed by this display of power and responded in faith to the Gospel.[110]

------

[110] Stanley, *Life Principles Bible, Acts 13:8-12*

Paul, Barnabas and John Mark sailed from Cyprus to Perga in Pamphylia on the mainland of Asia Minor. It was here that John Mark 'left Paul and Barnabas and returned to Jerusalem.'[111] Two major changes also occurred in the first mission at this juncture:

- Paul assumed the leading role in ministry; note the mention of "Barnabas and *Saul*," up to this point in scripture, changed to "Paul."[112]

- After St. Luke designated Saul as "Paul" for the first time in the Book of Acts, St. Luke changed 'Barnabas and Paul' to "Paul and his companions."[113] Hereafter, the name Paul is used to describe the apostle's work among the Gentiles, but even at this juncture, the name 'Saul' was used in the presence of Jews as it was more acceptable in those social environs.

After arriving in the port city of Perga, Paul and his companions trekked inland to the city of Pisidian Antioch. Here, Paul's message presented the ministry of Jesus Christ as fulfilled '*by prophecy*.'[114] In the synagogue on the Sabbath he spoke to his fellow Jews and laid out the history of the Jews from their forty years in the wilderness through the reigns of King Saul and David and from David and his descendants, the lineage leading up to Christ; "From the descendants of this man, according to promise, God has brought to Israel a Savior, Jesus."[115]

Paul ended his first visit to Pisidian Antioch with an appeal for his listeners to avoid the errors of some Jerusalem Jews who rejected Jesus as the messiah. Jews and proselytes did respond to Paul's message and 'begged' him to return on the following sabbath.

---

[111] Ibid. *Acts 13:13*.

[112] Ibid. Acts 13:9.

[113] Ibid. Acts 13:13

[114] Ibid. Isaiah 52:13-15, 53.

[115] Ibid. Acts 13:23-25.

Paul and Barnabas did return on the next sabbath and 'nearly the whole city assembled to hear the word of the Lord.'[116] In the assembly there were Jews (Judaizers – not Pharisees but *sticklers* for the Torah and Jewish Laws) who challenged the apostles and wanted them to leave. On the other hand, the Gentiles rejoiced at the 'good news' spoken by Paul. Paul admonished the Judaizers and told the assembly:

> "For so the Lord has commanded us, 'I HAVE PLACED YOU AS A LIGHT FOR THE GENTILES, THAT YOU MAY BRING SALVATION TO THE ENDS OF THE EARTH.'"[117]

'The Gentiles began glorifying the word of the Lord, and many believed and rejoiced having been saved with the promise of eternal life. And the word of the Lord was being spread through the whole region.' [118]

The Judaizers with help of the Jewish women threatened to instigate a persecution against Paul and Barnabas and drove them out of their district. Paul and Barnabas responded by 'shaking off the dust on their feet and left for Iconium.'[119]

A pattern formed in Pisidian Antioch - preaching the Gospel (starting in the synagogue), success with the Gentiles, encountering Jewish opposition, trying to engage more with the Gentiles, possibly facing persecution, departing – this is what Paul faced everywhere he traveled. '*The Way*' was a completely new movement and ministry and obviously the Gentiles saw 'a new hope' as never before. The 'Orthodox Jews' became increasingly alarmed with this 'new gospel' as it countered the Torah and Jewish Law. Paul's

---

[116] Ibid. Acts 13:44.

[117] Stanley, *Life Principles Bible, Acts 13:45-47.*

[118] Ibid. Acts 13:48,49.

[119] Ibid. Acts 13:51.

message was one of love from God bringing peace and redemption to those who never believed such a thing was possible; it was a message of rejoicings. Authors Lea and Black summed up Paul's future very succinctly:

> *"Wherever Paul evangelized, either a revival or rebellion followed."[120]*

The next stop was Iconium and its synagogue. Again, large numbers of people listened; some believed, some did not. The Judaizers did their best to 'embitter the minds of the Gentiles,' and when Paul and Barnabas heard there may be an attempt to 'mistreat and possibly stone them,' they left for cities in the Lycaonia region, Lystra and Derbe.[121]

Lycaonia was a large region in the interior of Asia Minor, north of the Tarsus Mountains. It was bounded on the east by Cappadocia, on the north by Galatia, and on the west by Phrygia and Pisidia. To the south, Lycaonia extended to the chain of Mount Taurus, where it bordered on the country popularly called, in earlier times Cilicia, and in the Byzantine period Isauria whose boundaries varied at different times.[122] Lycaonia lay in the core of the Taurus Mountains.

After leaving Iconium, Paul and Barnabas crossed the frontier and arrived at the city of Lystra. Never intimidated Paul continued to spread the Gospel in the synagogues and to Gentile listeners.

One of Paul's first encounters in Lystra was with a man who was lame. Paul noticed the man was listening intently and 'believed.'

---

[120] Thomas D. Lea and David Alan Black, *The New Testament: Its Background and Message (Nashville: B & H Academic, 2003), p. 345.*

[121] Stanley, *Life Principles Bible, Acts 14:1–8.*

[122] "Isauria," *Wikipedia,* https://en.wikipedia.org/wiki/Isauria. *Accessed January 9, 2020.*

Paul, in a loud voice said, "Stand up on your feet!" The man walked.[123] The pagan crowd was amazed and said these men had come as humans but were gods; Barnabas as Zeus and Paul as Hermes. A priest in a local temple associated with Zeus came to offer blessings and a sacrifice.

Paul and Barnabas when hearing what the locals were saying and insinuating, 'tore off their robes, walked into the crowds and said, "we are but men like yourselves and are teaching a true gospel of the one true living God WHO MADE THE HEAVEN AND THE EARTH AND THE SEA AND ALL THAT IS IN THEM. In the generations gone by He permitted all the nations to go their own ways: and yet He did not leave Himself without a witness, in that He did good and gave you rains from heaven and fruitful seasons, satisfying your hearts with food and gladness."[124] 'Paul reminded them their focus should be on their relationship with the living God.'[125]

Again, Judaizers from Iconium and Antioch followed Paul, stirred up the crowd, dragged Paul from the city and 'stoned him,' leaving him for dead. Obviously, Paul recovered quickly; he and Barnabas left for Derbe.[126]

After a stay in Derbe, Paul and Barnabas made a 'U-Turn' and made their way back visiting all the churches they had established apparently with no major 'trials or tribulations.' In the new church congregations, they helped with the 'appointment of elders' who would oversee the congregations with 'living in Christ' and the teachings of St. Paul and Barnabas.

Paul and Barnabas made-it back to Perga and set sail to Attalia, and from there back to Selucia, finally arriving at their home

---

[123] Stanley, *Life Principles Bible, Acts 14:9,10.*

[124] Ibid. Act 14: 14-16.

[125] Ibid. LIFE LESSONS, Acts 14:15, p. 1284.

[126] Ibid. Acts 14: 19-21.

church in Antioch. The mission was a two-year venture from AD 47 AD- to 49 (50) and covered approximately 1,235 miles. Upon their return to the church at Antioch, members rejoiced at the excitement of the Gentile believers whom they visited and were led to believe in the Lord. The mission was a success as God wanted Paul and Barnabas to concentrate on Gentile believers, and their expectations were 'more than met.'

Chapter 6 Study Questions

1. Where was Paul's 'Home Church?' How do you think Paul ended up in Antioch Syria?

2. Who accompanied Paul during his first mission?

3. Paul followed a protocol when entering a new city to preach the Gospel; what were the steps?

4. After Paul evangelized in each city, what were the opinions and receptions from those to whom Paul preached?

5. During Paul's first mission, he found the Gentiles were responding to his message favorably? Why was that important?

6. What is a Judaizer?

Chapter 7

POTENTIAL TROUBLE IN JERUSALEM THE JERUSALEM COUNCIL

The Antioch church did not impose strict conditions on the Gentile believers concerning the Mosaic Law. Pharisees who made a trip to Antioch from Judea but had converted to Christianity still believed the Gentiles should pay more attention to the Jewish Laws, especially those concerning '*circumcision.*' Paul and Barnabas argued their point as well with the brethren who were visiting from Jerusalem, and there was dissention amongst the two sides.

Another point of contention was the Judaizers from Jerusalem were disconcerted with the Jewish Christians in Antioch concerning the 'food laws' as spelled out in the Mosaic Laws. There may have been an atmosphere of hostility as the Judaizers even separated themselves from the Antioch brethren during meals. At this point, Paul may have been further formulating his gospel of Christ as he was serious in his 'appointment' to deliver the Gospel to the Gentiles, and that *didn't* include the Gentiles taking ownership of Jewish Law. 'God shows no partiality when one has accepted Jesus Christ as Savior, whether Orthodox Jew or Gentile.'[127]

---

[127] James D. G. Dunn, *The New Perspective on Paul (William G Eerdmans Publishing Company, Grand Rapids, MI, 2008), pp.188-191.*

The elders in the church decided it would be wise for Paul and Barnabas go to the apostles in Jerusalem and 'iron out differences' and receive better clarity on the issues at hand. The trip to Jerusalem occurred in the latter part of 49 AD, and during their journey, they took the opportunity to prophesize to new legions of non-believers in Samaria and Phoenicia 'describing in detail the conversion of the Gentiles and bringing great joy to all the brethren.'[128]

When Paul and Barnabas arrived in Jerusalem, they were welcomed by the church, the apostles and elders. They related their two-year mission and told how joyful the Gentile believers became when learning they could directly be included in *the family of God* without conversion to Judaism. Still there was a sect of Pharisee believers who stood up saying, 'It is necessary to circumcise them and to direct them to observe the Laws of Moses;'[129] the apostles and elders came together to seek a solution to this matter.

'Many of the Jewish Christians, those called Judaizers thought Gentile believers should be required to keep the Law in order to attain salvation (Acts 15:1,5). To answer those claims, the elders called the first conference of the early church called the *Jerusalem Council*. In that meeting, the leaders affirmed the truth: *"we don't have to earn our salvation through works or keeping the law - Christ has given it to us freely."*[130] Peter, a leading apostle (one of the original twelve) in Jerusalem stood up and said:

> "Brethren, you know in the early days God made a choice among you, that by my mouth the Gentiles would hear the word of the Gospel and believe. And God, who knows the heart, testified in them giving them the *'Holy Spirit'* just as He did us; and He made no distinction between us and them, cleansing their

---

[128] Stanley, *Life Principles Bible, Acts 15:3.*

[129] Stanley, *Life Principles Bible, Acts 15:5.*

[130] Stanley, *Life Principles Bible, LIFE LESSONS, Acts 15:11, p. 1285.*

heart by faith. Now, therefore why do you put God to the test by placing upon the neck of the disciples a yoke which neither our fathers nor we have been able to bear? But we believe that we are saved through the grace of the Lord Jesus, in the same way as they also are."[131]

Again, Paul and Barnabas spoke and were allowed to relate what signs and wonders God had done among the Gentiles. Afterwards, James, the brother of Jesus spoke to the council. He spoke with the words of the Prophets saying *that when Jesus returns, He will rebuild the Tabernacle of David which had fallen, and rebuild the ruins and restore it, so the best of mankind may seek the Lord, and all the Gentiles who are called by my Name. Therefore, it is my judgment that we do not trouble those who are turning to God from among the Gentiles, but that we write to them that they abstain from things contaminated by idols and from fornication and from what is strangled and from blood.*"[132]

It was decided by the council that a letter be sent to the church in Antioch relating what had been discussed and agreed upon to settle everyone's mind. Two of the elders from Jerusalem, Silas and Judas, also being disciples were to accompany Paul and Barnabas to encourage and explain the letter to the brethren in Antioch. Silas remained in Antioch and would later accompany Paul on his second missionary journey.

Despite the agreement achieved at the Jerusalem Council, Paul recounts how he later publicly confronted Peter in a dispute sometimes called the *"Incident at Antioch,"* over Peter's reluctance

---

[131] Ibid. Acts 15: 7-12.

[132] Ibid. Acts 15: 13-29.

to share a meal with Gentile Christians in Antioch because they did not strictly adhere to Jewish customs.[133]

Writing later of the incident, Paul recounts, "I opposed [Peter] to his face, because he was clearly in the wrong", and says to Peter, "You are a Jew, yet you live like a Gentile and not like a Jew. How is it, then, that you force Gentiles to follow Jewish customs?" (Galatians 2:11-14) Paul also mentions that even Barnabas, his traveling companion and fellow apostle until that time, sided with Peter. The outcome of the incident remains uncertain.[134]

Chapter 7 Study Questions

1. What was the purpose of the Jerusalem Council?

2. What was the role of Paul and Barnabas?

3. Why was Paul and Barnabas so excited about telling the Council about their first mission?

4. What role did Peter play at the council?

5. What role did James, the brother of Jesus play at the Jerusalem Council?

---

[133] Herbermann, Charles George, ed. (1910). "Judaizers," *The Catholic Encyclopedia: An International Work of Reference on the Constitution, Doctrine, Discipline, and History of the Catholic Church. 8. Infamy–Lapperent: New York: Robert Appleton Company. pp 537-538.*
[134] Ibid. pp. 537-538.

PAUL'S SECOND MISSIONARY JOURNEY

The second missionary journey began in late AD 49 AD or early AD 50. Paul and Barnabas remained at the church in Antioch and ministered to the members and new converts. Paul ready for a new mission invited Barnabas to accompany him as Paul wanted to visit the churches established during their first mission and strengthen the faith of the believers. The two apostles did agree on a second mission but had a 'sharp disagreement' on a possible role for John Mark who left them after landing in Perga and returned to Jerusalem during the first mission. As mentioned, John Mark was related to Barnabas, and he saw 'potential' in Mark; something Paul couldn't see.

Paul and Barnabas could not reach an agreement or compromise on John Mark, so the two men separated. From this split, two missionary journeys commenced: one with Barnabas and John Mark sailing back to Cyprus, and the other with Paul, and a new apostle from the Antioch Church, *Silas*. Even though John Mark did not accompany Paul, the two men continued to spread the Gospel to the Gentiles, and they did communicate with one another throughout their lives. It should be noted again John Mark wrote the Book of Mark, a synoptic gospel.[135]

The second missionary journey covered more than three thousand miles and lasted to the late winter in AD 53-54 including Paul's trip back to Caesarea and back to Antioch. Paul and Silas headed north (on foot) through Syria and Cilicia where again they strengthened and encouraged new believers; they did make a brief stop in Tarsus.

Paul and Silas continuing their journey visited the cities of Derbe and Lystra in southern Galatia in the Lycaonia region. As we may recall, it was in Lystra during his first mission, Paul was 'stoned and left for dead.'

During this visit, Paul added a 'new team member from Lystra, *'Timothy'* and would work closely and communicate with him for the rest of 'their lives.' Timothy was the son of a Jewish mother and Gentile father. To facilitate Timothy's acceptance into the ministry among the Jews, Paul (through resources at the synagogue) had Timothy circumcised.   'Whenever doctrinal issues were not at stake, Paul was willing to be flexible to encourage the spread of the Gospel.'[136] However, if any practice may have endangered the truth of the Gospel, Paul was adamant in his refusal to yield.[137] Even though Paul had relaxed his standards on Jewish law, especially that of circumcision, I can only hypothesize there were times when 'following the law may have benefited their ministry.' For purposes of appearances, Timothy was circumcised according to Jewish custom and possibly for that reason (or not), Timothy

---

[135] Charles F. Stanley, "The Gospel According to Mark," *Life Principles Bible, New American Standard Bible (La Habra, CA: Lockman Foundation, 2009), p.1149.*

[136] Stanley, *Life Principles Bible, 1 Corinthians. 9:19-23.*

[137] Ibid. Galatians 1:6-9.

was practicing Jewish law which may have helped appease current and future Judaizers.[138]

Paul, Silas and Timothy, after leaving Lystra and visiting Iconium for a second time, embarked on a long leg of this mission through southern Galatia and Phrygia. According to scripture they were "forbidden by the Holy Spirit to speak the word" in Asia.[139] 'After coming to Mysia and planning to visit Bithynia, the "Spirit of Jesus" did not permit them; passing by Mysia, they eventually came to Troas.'[140]

Soon after, 'Paul and his companions' *developed* a strategy for evangelism they arranged to follow, but they never let their plans get in the way of the Spirit's leading. Obeying the Lord's direction, they crossed the Aegean Sea and entered new territory – *Europe* – with the gospel. Paul later planted churches in Philippi, Thessalonica, and Berea which would prove to be very strategic in the spread of Christianity.[141] There is little information concerning this part of the trek, and the party finally arrived in Troas.

Troas

After Paul arrived in Troas, '*a vision*' appeared to him at night of a man from Macedonia standing and appealing to him to "come over to Macedonia and help us;" this known as the 'Macedonia vision.' Other than 'the vision interpreted as a call for help,' Paul had no other reason to visit the district of Macedonia.[142] On several occasions Paul had *visions* from God; he prayed, listened and obeyed. Most visions kept Paul and his companions out of harm's

---

[138] Ibid. Acts 16:3.

[139] Ibid. Acts 16:6.

[140] Ibid. Acts 16:7,8.

[141] Ibid. LIFE LESSONS, Acts 16:6,7. p. 1286.

[142] Ibid. Acts 16:9.

way such as those he had on his future sea voyage from Judea to Rome after the third mission and trials in Caesarea.

Immediately, Paul and companions sailed from Troas on a straight course to Samothrace, and on the following day to Neapolis eventually arriving in Philippi. Philippi was a colony in Macedonia where many Roman war veterans could retire and live under Roman law with freedom from taxes.

Philippi

Philippi was a city with few Jews and lacking the number of Jewish men and families to build a synagogue. While in Philippi, a woman who sold purple fabrics named *Lydia* listened and believed in Paul's message of the Gospel. She was baptized along with her household and was also the *'first convert in Europe.'* Lydia also prevailed on Paul to come to her home and stay during his visit.[143]

There were two other noteworthy occurrences involving Paul and Silas while in Philippi. The first centered on a slave girl who would collect money for 'telling fortunes.' She was controlled by two 'managers' (masters) for whom she worked. Having followed Paul and Silas for days and crying out, 'These men are bond-servants of the "most High God," who are proclaiming to you the way of salvation.' She became somewhat of an annoyance to Paul, and he called out to the 'malevolent spirit in her soul' and commanded, "In the name of Jesus Christ, leave," and the spirit "immediately left."

Of course, the two masters lost their source of income and were greatly angered; they 'seized and dragged' Paul and Silas to a town assembly and before chief magistrates exclaiming they were "proclaiming customs" unlawful for Romans to hear and causing a frenzy amongst citizens. The chief magistrates in turn 'tore off

---

[143] Stanley, *Life Principles Bible, Acts 16:14,15.*

the robes of Paul and Silas' and had them beaten with rods before throwing them into a maximum - security cell.[144] (Over the course of Paul's travels, he was beaten with rods three times, and 'whipped by the Jews five times' sustaining "forty – minus – one lashing, each").[145] Both Paul and Silas were Roman citizens and should have had a hearing and day in court before any beatings as *it was illegal to punish a Roman citizen without a trial.*

Without a doubt, the beatings left both Paul and Silas exhausted, and they found themselves in a dirty, dark and foul-smelling inner cell. 'Silas did not meditate on injustice nor despaired of his situation. Instead, faith filled his heart, and when Paul and Silas lifted their voices in song and praise, a violent earthquake shook the prison (earthquakes in this region are numerous and often severe). The doors were flung open and the restraints loosened.'[146]

They did not try to escape or run. If a prisoner escaped from a Roman prison, it was customary for the jailer to be executed. The jailer awakened to survey the damage, assumed the prisoners had escaped and considered taking his own life, but Paul called out to him and assured him they remained in jail. The jailer "called for lights and led them out" asking the apostles "what he must do to be saved." They said, "Believe in the Lord Jesus, and you will be saved and your household." The jailer did take them into his home, cleaned their wounds and fed them.

The following day, the magistrates sent guards to release Paul and Silas after learning they were Roman citizens telling them they 'were allowed to go their way.' 'But Paul said to them, "They have beaten us in public without trial, men who are Romans, and have thrown us into

---

[144] Ibid. Acts 16:22-24.

[145] Ibid. Acts 16: 22-23.

[146] Stanley, *Life Principles Bible, Life Examples: Silas, Acts 16:24-34. p.1287.*

prison; and now are they sending us away secretly? No indeed! But, let them come themselves and bring us out."[147]

The magistrates came and were very concerned at their indiscretion and lack of justice for Roman citizens. They also appealed and "begged" Paul and Silas to 'please leave the city.' When they were released, they went back to the home of Lydia and encouraged the brethren to keep the faith alive; soon afterwards Paul and Silas departed.

Thessalonica

Paul and companions continued their journey through Macedonia and went to the city of Thessalonica, the capital of Macedonia. He stayed true to his evangelical strategy of ministering in the synagogue and to Gentile believers in homes where he lodged.

"The city of Thessalonica was founded in 315 BC by Cassander, a General of Alexander the Great. He named the city after his wife Thessalonica, the daughter of Philip of Macedon and the sister of Alexander."[148] Thessalonica, a major seaport, experienced faster than normal population growth, and when Paul visited the city, its population may have been as high as two-hundred thousand. Paul's initial ministry is narrated in Acts 17:4-9. He preached the Gospel for three consecutive Sabbaths, and again Paul encountered the typical hostility among unbelieving Jews (Judaizers).

A man named Jason hosted Paul and his associates while in Thessalonica. Unfortunately, the crowd of disbelieving Jews caught up with Jason and Paul, attacked Jason's home and accused them of civil unrest and treason. Local authorities stepped in and calmed the situation. Jason was directed to 'pledge a bond' while Paul was in Thessalonica and expressed that it would be a 'good idea if Paul left town.' The local brethren spirited Paul out of town at night.

---

[147] Ibid. Acts 16:37.

[148] Thomas D. Lea and David Alan Black, *The New Testament: Its Background and Message (Nashville: B & H Publishing Group, 2003) p. 377.*

Berea

Paul, Silas, and Timothy immediately walked to Berea. Veria, officially transliterated "Veroia," historically also spelled "Berea," is a city in northern modern Greece located 317 miles north-northwest of Athens and 45 miles west-southwest of Thessalonica.[149] Beria is one of the oldest cities in ancient Greece; its founding dating back to 1000 BC. Possibly best known for textiles and agriculture during the time of Paul, Berea also had lignite mines in the vicinity. Lignite, a very low grade of coal (brown coal), is compressed peat and has a low heat output.

The Berean Jews were very receptive to Paul's message. They had studied Old Testament scripture and were looking forward to Paul's visit. Again, Paul had issues in Berea as Thessalonian Judaizers followed Paul and stirred up the locals. The Berean brethren and followers help Paul move south, recommending he go to the seacoast, and that meant traveling to the next large city which happened to be Athens. Silas and Timothy stayed behind, but later joined Paul in Athens 'at his command,' thus leaving Berea also.[150]

Athens

Upon his arrival, Paul noted, as had many who traveled through Athens, the city was *inundated* with idols. He may have arrived in mid – to late AD 51. Over time, Paul enjoyed his stay and found Athens to be a world center of culture, intelligence, and wisdom. A 'college town' of sorts, Athens had its fair share of eminent world philosophers who taught in the institutes of higher learning and understanding. At that time in history, Jerusalem was the center

---

[149] "Veria," *Wikipedia, last modified February 4, 2017, accessed April 3, 2017, https://en.wikipedia.org/wiki/Veria/.*

[150] Stanley, *Life Principles Bible, Acts 17:14,15.*

of the true Judean belief- religion, Rome, the center of the imperial authority, and Athens, the intellectual center of the world.

Paul noted the numerous idols and statues in the city, and there were streets where homes had a pillar with the bust of the Greek god Hermes; the historian Pliny the Elder wrote 'there were more than three thousand statues within the city.' Paul did find one altar that was inscribed to the *"Unknown God"* which he effectively used as a basis for developing and preaching the Gospel about the 'One True God and Jesus Christ.'

Keeping to his agenda, Paul delivered his message of the Gospel to the Jews and "God-fearing Gentiles" in-and around the synagogues. He was out amongst citizenry that included Epicurean and Stoic philosophers, daily. 'Some philosophers were very interested in what he had to say; some were saying, "What would *this idle babbler* wish to say?" Others, "He seems to be a proclaimer of strange deities," as he was preaching about Jesus and the resurrection.'[151]

Paul was offered an opportunity in Athens he had not experienced before. The Athenians said, "For you are bringing some strange things to our ears; we want to know what these things mean." They took and brought him to the *Areopagus* on Mars Hill or the Hill of Ares saying, "May we know what this new teaching is which you are proclaiming." Many Athenians and strangers visiting Athens used to spend their time in nothing other than telling or hearing something new.[152]

This may have been an informal setting, or possibly a quasi-court setting to examine Paul's teachings. Paul acknowledged the truth of some philosophical ideas, particularly of the Stoics, but

---

[151] Stanley, *Life Principles Bible, Acts 17:17,18.*
[152] Ibid. Acts 17:19-21.

suggested that *those thinkers* had not gone far enough. 'Paul stood in their midst of the Areopagus and said,

"Men of Athens, I observe that you are very religious in all respects. For while I was passing through and examining the objects of your worship, I also found an altar with this inscription,

'TO AN UNKNOWN GOD'

Therefore, what you worship in ignorance, this I proclaim to you. The God who made the world and all things in it, since He is Lord of the heaven and earth, does not dwell in temples made with hands; nor is He served by human hands, as though He needed anything, since He Himself gives *to all people* life and breath and all things; and He made from one *man* every nation of mankind to live on all the face of the earth, having determined *their* appointed times and the boundaries of habitation, that they seek God, if perhaps might grope for Him and find Him, though He is not far from each one of us;"[153] (Paul knew that the Athenians were searching for truth, so he explained that God had revealed Himself to mankind through nature and history so that we would know that He exists and would be without excuse (Romans 1:20),[154] "for in Him we live and move and exist, as even some of your poets have said, 'For we are also His children.'"

"Being then the children of God, we ought not to think that the Divine Nature is like gold or silver or stone, an image formed by the image and thought of man. Therefore, having overlooked the times of ignorance,

---

[153] Stanley, *Life Principles Bible, Acts 17: 22-27.*
[154] Ibid. LIFE LESSONS, Acts 17:27, p.1289.

God is now declaring to men that *all people* everywhere should repent, *because He has fixed a day in which He will judge the world in righteousness through a Man whom He appointed, having finished proof to all men by raising him from the dead.*"[155]

After his speech, some believed, others intrigued, but there were those that merely 'sneered,' "So Paul went out of their midst."[156] As to Athens, there seemed to be 'no forced exit, no Judaizers to any extent, nor was he asked to leave.' Athens was a good *different* experience for Paul. Athens, a city of engrained intellectual curiosity with a constant flow of new people was a perfect setting for Paul to deliver the Gospel.

Corinth

Paul arrived in Corinth for the first time in AD 51 - through AD 52. Corinth was then a little more than one-hundred years old but had a population five times that of Athens. It was both a strategic and commercial seaport municipality. Paul, realized the importance of the city and seaport for the entire Roman Empire as "it was a magnet for a diversity of people traveling east-west, and north-south."[157]

In 146 BC the Roman consul Lucius Mummius Achaicus crushed the uprising in Corinth of the Achaean Confederacy against Roman rule in Greece, leveled the city, killing all the men, and sold women and children into slavery.[158] For the next one hundred years, Corinth was occupied by 'squatters.' It wasn't until 44 BC

---

[155] Ibid. Acts 17:28-31.

[156] Ibid. Acts 17:33.

[157] Dan P. Cole, "Corinth and Ephesus," December 1998, accessed April 3, 2017, *Biblical Archaeology Society (BAS Library), https://members.bib-arch.org/ bible-review/4/6/6.*

[158] "Lucius Mummius,' www.britannica.com/biography/Lucius Mummius.

that Julius Caesar rebuilt the city and named it Colonia Laus Julia Corinthiensis, and reoccupied the city with conscripted Italian, Greek, Syrian, Egyptian and Judean 'free slaves' consequently laying a basis for diverse belief systems and religions.

Corinth was an enormously wealthy commerce center. There were two seaports in proximity to one another, and the seaports sat on the crossroads of many nations, provinces and regions of the Roman Empire. The city also drew many self-made men and women from all over the region.[159]

Corinth also had a *dubious well-known* underside. The city had a reputation for fast profligate living. Realizing the costliness and moral turpitude involved in visiting Corinth, the Roman geographer Strabo coined what became an ancient proverb for the city: "*Not for every man is the voyage to Corinth.*"[160] Moralists used the name of the city to coin the Greek verb *kiorinthiazesthai*, whose definition means "to practice fornication."[161] Building a church in this loose, licentious city would be no easy task; immorality, contentiousness, heresy, and brutality were all prevalent in this prosperous pagan community.

Another group of visitors who came to Corinth were those to watch and participate in the *Isthmian Games* which were held every two years and occurred during the summer of AD 51 when Paul lived there. Like the better-known games at Olympia, the Isthmian Games were 'Panhellenic' attracting athletes and spectators from Greek settlements throughout the Mediterranean. Corinth would certainly provide Paul with multiple opportunities to reach many and spread the Gospel.

---

[159] J. E. Harry, "Corinth in the Bible," accessed April 3, 1017, *Biblical History Online, www.bible-history.com/isbe/c/CORINTH.*

[160] Cole, "Corinth and Ephesus."

[161] Lea and Black, *The New Testament, 403.*

Aquila and Priscilla

Paul had an affinity to the city of Corinth; he resided there for eighteen months. Soon after arriving, he made the acquaintance of two citizens that was eventful developing into a friendship lasting a lifetime. "He found a Jew named *Aquila* of Pontus, having recently come from Italy with his wife *Priscilla* because Emperor Claudius (AD 45 – 54) had commanded all the Jews to leave Rome.

Paul came to them and being a tent maker, he stayed with them, and they were working together, "for by trade *they* were tent-makers."[162] Just as the foundation of the first church in Europe located in Philippi developed and Paul's relationship with Lydia had developed, Paul had the fortune to meet Priscilla and her husband, Aquila (the "Eagle").

In Romans, Paul writes that Priscilla and Aquila were lifelong 'best friends,' and mentions, "They worked with me in Christ Jesus, and risked their necks for my life, to whom not only do I give thanks, but also all the churches of the Gentiles.'"[163] Priscilla and Aquila were but two of many lifelong friends of Paul; others included Timothy, Titus, Silas, Barnabas, John Mark and St. Luke who accompanied Paul on the second mission.

Paul became in a sense, a business associate of Priscilla and Aquila. Clubs and voluntary associations of tradespeople were one the distinctive social structures during that time in Corinth. Juvenal, the Roman satirist blamed much of the immorality and superstition of that age on the fact that women found emancipation through these clubs – Priscilla belonged to this social stratum. (It may be an opportune time to qualify Juvenal as a critic of the times. He lived in the latter half of the first century and into the second century AD. Juvenal was a poet and writer of satire).

[162] Stanley, *Life Principles Bible, Acts 18:2,3.*
[163] Ibid. Romans 16:3,4.

Luke mentions Priscilla and Aquila were Jews. Whether they moved from mainstream Judaism to Paul's persuasion, or whether Paul converted them from being *Ebionite*, is unknown. Ebionites were portrayed as traditional Jews who zealously followed the Laws of Moses, revered Jerusalem as the holiest city, and restricted table fellowship only with Jews and Gentiles who had converted to Judaism. It is not known whether it was in Priscilla and Aquila's home, or in the home of another wealthy Corinthian the first Christians gathered for religious worship. It is no exaggeration to speculate the church in Corinth may have started as a 'business club' amongst leatherworkers and tentmakers. The clubs were especially advantageous to women who could trade 'in their own right' with the support of like-minded trading communities.

After residing with Priscilla and Aquila for a time, Paul moved to the home of a Gentile God-fearing man named *Titus Justus*, who fortunately lived next door to a synagogue. Paul also befriended *Crispus*, the leader of the synagogue, and after hearing Paul, he and his household became believers. Paul, from day one was ministering in the synagogue as that was his 'modus operandi.' "He was reasoning in the synagogue every Sabbath trying to persuade Jews and Greeks, but when Silas and Timothy came down from Macedonia, Paul began devoting himself completely to the word, solemnly testifying to the Jews and Greeks that Jesus was the Christ and Messiah. But when they resisted and blasphemed, he shook out his garments and said to them, 'Your blood *be* on your heads! I am clean. From now on I will go to the Gentiles.'"[164]

Again, Paul was harassed by Judaizers in Corinth, and again he experienced *another vision* from the Lord:

> "Do not be afraid *any* longer but go on speaking and
> do not be silent; for I am with you, for I have many
> people in this city."[165]

---

[164] Stanley, *Life Principles Bible, Acts 18:4-8.*
[165] Ibid. Acts 18:9,10.

The Judaizers eventually 'rose up and brought' Paul before the Roman proconsul of Achaia, *Gallio*. Gallio was the older brother on Seneca, the Roman stoic philosopher who first tutored and later counseled Nero, the future Roman Emperor. In AD 52, the Roman Senate appointed Gallio the governor or "proconsul" of the Roman Senatorial province of "Achaia" whose capital was Corinth.[166]

The Judaizers claimed, "This man persuades men to worship God contrary to the law." But when Paul was about to open his mouth, Gallio said to the Jews, "If it were a matter of wrong or of a vicious crime, O Jews, it would be reasonable for me to put up with you, but if there is a question about words and names and your own law, look after it yourselves; I am unwilling to be a judge of these matters."[167] Gallio's decision was *very important and set a precedent* as governors and proconsuls throughout the region decided that unless an offense was very egregious, or of a vicious nature, a proconsul was to have nothing to do with Jewish matters.

Gallio's ruling did not set-well with the Jews. "Then all the Greeks took *Sosthenes*, the ruler of the synagogue and "ringleader of the Jews" (who succeeded Crispus) and beat him before the judgment seat (with 'rods or 39 lashes'); Gallio paid no attention. Instead of Paul and the Christians being punished, the persecutor of Paul and Christians was punished.[168]

After this incident, Paul remained in Corinth a while longer. When he left, Paul and companions, including Priscilla and Aquila set sail for Asia Minor, and went to the city of Ephesus.

Again, entering the synagogue and trying to reason with the Jews he may or may not have had any noteworthy encounters. The believers wanted Paul to remain in Ephesus, but he did not

---

[166] "Gallio," bibleversestudy.com/acts/acts18-gallio.htm.

[167] Stanley, *Life Principles Bible, Acts 18:13-15.*

[168] Stanley, *Life Principles Bible, Acts 18:17.*

consent, but when leaving them, he said, "I will return to you again if God wills." He sailed from Ephesus back to Caesarea, greeting the church, and finally left for Antioch.[169]

Chapter 8 Study Questions

1. Silas accompanied Paul during his second mission; how did Paul and Silas become acquainted?

2. Paul and Silas left on the second mission by foot and visited the churches Paul had visited during his first mission. Why was this important?

3. How would you describe Paul's visit in Philippi?

4. After Paul visited Athens and Corinth, how did Paul change his strategy when moving from city–to city?

5. Priscilla and Aquila became life-long friends of Paul. What were traits, and why may they have bonded upon meeting one another?

6. Who was Gallio, and why was his judgment important to Paul and believers?

---

[169] Ibid. Acts 18:18-22.

THE FIRST LETTERS OF ST. PAUL GALATIANS 1 & 2 THESSALONIANS

In the story and history of Paul, it may be the appropriate time to look at three letters written to the believers in two of the churches he founded during the first two missions: *Galatians, 1 Thessalonians, and 2 Thessalonians.* In Galatians, he strongly urges a new and young assembly to believe in the Gospel of Jesus Christ as delivered and ministered by him versus listening and accepting views of the Judaizers and fostering the Jewish law.

The Thessalonian church assembly was a newly established church experiencing growing pains. It needed the type of 'parental love' Paul always extended to the Thessalonians. Paul also addresses the Judaizers and others who did not accept his new Gospel.

When reading the New Testament, after the Book of Acts comes the Book of Romans as Paul's letters, and others *were not written* in chronological order but positioned in the New Testament according to length. The Book of Romans is the longest written letter, circa AD 57, while the shortest is to a fellow Christian, *Philemon*, circa AD 60-62 while Paul was a prisoner in Rome (or possible incarceration in Ephesus). If looking at a timeline of Paul's activities and writings, one will notice his first three Epistles were directed to churches as a whole – *the body of Christ*, the church assemblies.

Galatians

There are two theories as to when Galatians was written. One 'unconfirmed' theory dates the letter prior to the completion of the Jerusalem Council. Perhaps the meeting described in Galatians 2:9,10 were preliminary private meetings held during the Jerusalem Council and prior to James announcement of the decisions at the Council. "Paul may have felt that the issues confronting the Galatians were so important he had to write his letter before the conclusion of the Council. If we follow the understanding of the incidents in Galatians and Acts, it may be possible to date the epistle as early as AD 49 AD – 50. These dates cannot be maintained with certainty."[170] I can only hypothesize; I do not know if the Galatians or their representatives could have sent Paul information as the Jerusalem Council started soon after he completed his mission.

After his second journey through the Galatian region, Paul may have got a 'first-hand look' as to *what was* going on and wrote the letter between AD 50 – 52. Another source even indicates the letters to the Thessalonians were the first, but if Galatians is first, it is the 'oldest epistle of the New Testament.' The Galatian's letter precedes the four Gospels by almost half century.

Soon after churches in the region of Galatia in Asia Minor were established, many Jews and Jewish Christians, again, questioned whether Gentile converts should be required to keep the traditions and laws of Judaism to attain salvation. This was 'similar to the idea of the *grace versus works*' debate fueled by the Judaizers in Jerusalem and the Antioch Church.[171] The Galatian letter basically "turned

[170] Lea and Black, *The New Testament: It's Background and Message (Nashville: B & H Publishing Group)*, 2003. P. 370
[171] Stanley, *Life Principle Bible, Acts 15.*

Judaism upside down." Paul was livid when he found out Judaizers had infiltrated the Galatian church and were trying to get the new Christians to abide by the Jewish laws in the Torah more so than the new theology of Christ (Christology). Paul's message, 'You cannot work your way into heaven with good works and abiding by the Torah. Paul strongly asserts, "and is not justified by works of the Law but through faith in Jesus Christ. The works of the Law, not flesh, *will be justified.*"[172]

Paul opened the door for both Gentiles and Jews to know that believing in Christ was their only 'ticket to salvation and eternal life.' He wanted the Galatians to know they could *not* find favor with God, but *God would find favor in them through Jesus Christ.* 'They would be "free from slavery of doubt to their salvation when they became free in Jesus."'[173]

Paul begins his letter as he did most of his future letters by establishing his credentials as an apostle who had *received his message and authority directly from "revelations of Christ."*[174] He wrote that blessings come from the Lord on the basis of obedience and faith, not adherence to rituals and laws. While the law declares people guilty and imprisons them, Jesus's *grace* sets people free to enjoy liberty eternally.

The entire opening of the letter was intended to say in effect, that whatever the Jerusalem leaders (Jerusalem Council) decided or did not, was beside the point since Paul's authority was from Christ, not from humankind. Paul goes on to argue that the Torah and law given to Israel in the time of Moses was only a 'temporary revelation' that had been annulled (but not totally dismissed) by

---

[172] Ibid. 15:11-12

[173] Stephen P. Eason, "Twelve Words of Hope for the World: Freedom," July 2, 2017. *First Presbyterian Church, Richmond, Virginia, www.fpcrichmond.org/ sermons.*

[174] James D. Tabor, *The Jesus Dynasty, p.241.*

the coming of Christ. He wrote, "The Torah was our tutor until Christ came, that we might be justified by faith. But now that faith has come, we are no longer under a tutor. For you are all sons of God through faith in Jesus."[175] Paul using the 'first person' here indicates that he as a Jew was also no longer under the law. Those with faith in Jesus Christ were part of a *new creation* in which the distinctions between being Jewish or Gentile were no longer valid.[176]

Paul makes clear that both Jews and Gentiles are descendants of Abraham. One needs to recognize "that Paul's reaction and views of *his* Judaism were not one of wholesale denunciation but was targeted against the misconception of the *role of works* in the process of salvation, the conventional nomism (the practice of religious legalism, basing the standards of good actions upon the moral law) excluded Gentiles from the process."[177]

He cautioned the believers 'this should not be interpreted as a license to sin.' On the contrary, believers are to maintain their freedom in Christ by "walking in His Spirit and produce the fruits of righteousness."[178] Paul emphasized that through the grace of Jesus, the Galatians are empowered to crucify "the flesh with its passions and desires (Gal. 5:24) and are able to please the Lord by living a godly, obedient lifestyle (Gal. 5:13,14)".

"O foolish Galatians!"[179] Paul urged the Galatians to consider the utter foolishness of trying to earn through their own efforts what had already been given to them by *the grace, power, and wisdom of God.*[180] [181] The grace of God cannot be attained by human

[175] Stanley, *Life Principles Bible, Galatians 3:24-26.*

[176] Tabor, *The Jesus Dynasty, p. 241.*

[177] Dunn, *The New Perspective on Paul, p.54*

[178] Stanley, *Life Principles Bible, Acts 5:16-25.*

[179] Ibid. Galatians 3:1.

[180] Ibid. Galatians 3:3.

[181] Ibid. Galatians 1:22,23.

endeavor; it can only be earned through a *faith-in and acceptance of Jesus Christ, the Son of God as their Savior.* Only by following Jesus's example and depending upon the Holy Spirit for strength and direction could they hope to once more experience the sheer joy they felt (experienced) at the beginning of their Christian walk.[182]

In Galatians 5:22-23 Paul describes the Spirit of God through metaphors using "fruits" (fruit of the Spirit) as a way of describing God's character, and as we know, fruits cannot be manufactured. The "fruit of the Spirit," the character of God in essence, grows within the believer as his or her faith and trust in God grows. The fruits of the Spirit are *love, joy, peace forbearance, kindness, goodness, faithfulness, gentleness and self-control.*[183] Paul further adds, "Against such things, *there is no law.*[184] Those who belong in Christ Jesus have crucified the flesh with its passions and desires. Since we live by the Spirit, let us keep *in step* with the Spirit. Let us not become conceited, provoking and envying each other.[185]

The large influx of Gentiles into the churches in Galatia made the theological issues Paul addressed enormously important. Had the views of Judaizers won the day, "then the gospel of salvation as a free gift from God received by faith would have seriously been undermined and compromised."[186]

First and Second Thessalonians

Paul wrote these letters to the Thessalonians circa AD 51-52, and the two letters are considered 'early letters.' There is a question

---

[182] Ibid. Galatians 4:15-20.

[183] Stanley, *Life Principles Bible, Galatians 5:22,23*

[184] Stephen P. Eason, "Fruit of the Spirit: Peace," June 26, 2016, accessed April 3, 2017, *First Presbyterian Church, Richmond, VA*, www.fpcrichmond. org/sermons, 2016.

[185] Stanley, *Life Principles Bible, Galatians 5:24-26.*

[186] F.F. Bruce, *Paul: Apostle of the Heart set Free, pp. 173-187.*

as to which letter was written and sent first, but they were likely written within months of one another.[187]

Even though Paul spent little time in Thessalonica during the second mission (a few weeks to a few months), he displayed a "parental love"[188] toward the new church. The church consisted of mainly Gentiles, and these converts were seemingly 'severely persecuted.'

The Thessalonians before Paul's arrival practiced a local religion that was established by a cult, *the Cabiri*. "The Cabeiri or Cabiri were a group of enigmatic chthonic deities (spirits, gods, deities *living under* the earth). These deities were worshiped in a mystery cult closely associated with that of Hephaestus, centered in the north Aegean Island of Lemnos and possibly Samothrace (at the Samothrace temple complex and at Thebes). In their distant origins the Cabeiri and the Samothracian gods may include pre-Greek elements or other non-Greek elements, such as Thracian, Tyrrhenian, Pelasgian, Phrygian or Hittite."[189] The Cabeiri was incorporated by the aristocracy and made into an official civil religion; *that left the working class feeling abandoned.* The resulting vacuum made Christianity particularly attractive to the Gentiles in Thessalonica.[190]

Thessalonica had become another city where the Judaizers made life for Paul and his companions. *difficult.* They did everything to discredit Paul's teachings and theology by telling the new church that Jesus had 'come and gone;' the Judaizers made Paul's mission more formidable. These were the ever-present Judaizers

---

[187] John P. Polhill, *Paul and His Letters*, *(Nashville: B & H Publishing Group, 1999), pp. 1187,188.*

[188] Stanley, *Life Principles Bible*, *"The First Epistle of Paul the Apostle to the Thessalonians," Introduction to the Books of Thessalonians, p. 1413.*

[189] Cabeiri – Wikipedia, en.wikipedia.org/wiki/Cabeiri.

[190] Pohill, *Paul and His Letters, p. 185.*

who infected the assemblies, and strongly opposed the 'teachings of Paul' and after his departure almost destroying what Paul and Timothy had put in place.

Once Paul's concern for the survival of the new church peaked, he sent Timothy back to mitigate the problems and assess the damages and encourage the young new believers to 'keep the faith.' Even with a few lingering concerns, Timothy returned and reported to Paul a positive analysis of the situation. The 'lingering concerns' may have prompted Paul to write the second letter to the Thessalonians.[191] Both Thessalonian letters deal with questions related to the Parousia (Second Coming of Christ) as the Thessalonians seem to have had questions and concerns surrounding that issue.[192]

First Thessalonians

In the first letter, Paul encouraged the new believers to excel in their newfound faith, to increase their love for one another, and to rejoice, pray and give thanks always. He ended chapters with the reminder that *the 'Lord is coming back.'*[193]

Paul reminded the church that Christ's Advent signals hope and comfort for all believers, living and dead. The fact that Paul emphasized the Lord's return to a young church assembly perhaps suggested the importance of teaching the doctrine of the Second Coming in a practical way so to lay a foundation for a mature Christian faith – Jesus rose from the dead, had 'eyewitnesses,' ascended to heaven and promised He would return again. Paul certainly did not know when but was convinced of a Second Coming – *the point Paul was driving home.*

---

[191] Stanley, *Life Principles Bible, p. 1413.*
[192] Polhill, p. 180.
[193] Lea and Black, *The New Testament, pp. 311-315.*

Paul had taught the Thessalonians his basics: accept Christ, baptize, and live a new life as Christ lived with the Holy Spirit dwelling in their hearts. Paul had fatherly love for the Thessalonians, but there is no biblical reference indicating *why* he felt this way (possibly the assembly was mostly Gentiles – other writers, researchers and theologians tend to concur). After the arrival of the first letter, additional seeds of false doctrine were being sown among the assembly causing them to waver in their faith. The second letter clarified many of the doctrinal issues that were causing distress.

Second Thessalonians

The letter begins by commending the believers on their faithfulness in the midst of persecution and encouraging them. Their present suffering will be repaid in far greater measure with the 'future glory,' therefore the assembly should live confidently and with hopeful expectations for a brighter future.

Paul then turns to the central matters of his second letter - correcting a misunderstanding regarding the *Second Coming*. False teachers were reporting that Christ had already returned to the church, and the Thessalonians essentially 'missed him.'

A small segment of the assembly was convinced Christ would return immediately, consequently believing it was 'no longer of any use to work.' Others took advantage of the church's practice of charity and interdependence, living off the wealth of others.[194] Paul emphasized their belief in the Second Coming did not give them an excuse to be lazy. "For, even when we were with you, we used to give you this order: if anyone is not willing to work, then he is not to eat, either."[195]

---

[194] Stanley, *Life Principles Bible, Acts 2:42-47.*
[195] Ibid. Thessalonians 3:10.

Paul assured the believers the Lord had not yet come, and they had not missed the Rapture. As evidence, he detailed the extraordinary events that would take place when Jesus comes:

- "The falling away of the church must occur."[196]

- "The man of lawlessness must be revealed." The extraordinary ruthless and wicked leader (or group of people) will completely rebel against the Lord's authority. The "man of lawlessness" is known by several names in scripture: *'The Antichrist, The beast, the son of perdition among them.'*

- "The restrainer must be removed from the earth." Who is the restrainer? Most likely the Holy Spirit at work in-and through the church.[197]

How were the Thessalonians to respond to this kind of prophecy? Paul admonished them to labor diligently for the Gospel until Christ returned, and in his theology of justification, wrote "those who lived by faith would realize a deep, heartfelt understanding of peace and joy."[198] I am also sure Paul had to remind the new church that *patience was a tremendous virtue* and that sticking to the tenets of this new ideology, Christianity, or "the Way," may take perseverance, and as always, he asked them to 'keep the faith.'

---

[196] Ibid. Thessalonians 2:3.

[197] Stanley, *Life Principles Bible, Thessalonians 2:6,7.*

[198] Irving L Brittle Jr., *It's Not Rocket Science – The Theology of St. Paul the Apostle (2nd edition) (Sheridan, WY: Pen House LLC. 2020), p.61.*

Chapter 9 Study Questions

1. What was happening at the churches in Galatia that was of concern to Paul?

2. What was the 'primary concern' of the assembly in Thessalonica?

3. How is the message of 2 Thessalonians 3:10 applicable to many in this day and time?

Chapter 10

THIRD MISSIONARY JOURNEY, AD 52-57

Paul set-off on his extended third missionary journey in mid-to late AD 52 from the Church in Antioch with companions. He took the overland route along the same roads and paths as those of the second journey heading to the city of Ephesus where his 'lifelong friends' lived, *Priscilla and Aquila.* Paul resided in Ephesus for two years,[199] and being a tentmaker and evangelist, he stayed busy in both endeavors. He encountered his recurring issues with Judaizers, and later, with artisan-merchants of Ephesus who sold 'miniatures (idols) of Artemis (Diana),' the fertility goddess.

Academics and theologians concur Ephesus was the most important city Paul visited and lived during his third mission. It is located at the intersection of two ancient major overland routes; the coastal road running north to Troas, and the western route to Colossae, Laodicea, and beyond to the western edge of Asia Minor (modern Turkey) with easy access to the Aegean Sea.

Ephesus

Ephesus had become a strategic city and a main crossroad either by land or sea from Rome to the east. Ephesus had a harbor during

---

[199] Stanley, *Life Principles Bible, Acts 19:10*

79

Paul's visit on the Cayster River known as "The Landing Place," and the citizens were proud of its role as a port and gateway city to Asia Minor. Unfortunately, the harbor filled with silt at the end of the first century causing some economic decline, but Ephesus remained a major political, commercial, and religious center.[200]

Apollos

Just as Paul arrived in Ephesus, another apostle, *Apollos had just left* for Corinth, and he did leave a contingency of disciples. Apollos was an Alexandrian by birth, and an "eloquent man, mighty in the Scriptures and instructed in the speaking and teaching 'accurately' the things concerning Jesus, being only acquainted with the baptism of John."[201] He is mentioned as a Christian teacher who had come to Ephesus in early AD 52.

Apollos "spoke out boldly in the synagogue" with Aquila and Priscilla in attendance. "But when they heard him, they took him aside and explained to him the way of God more accurately."[202] Although he had learned many things about Jesus, he did not fully understand what Christ had done through His death and resurrection. "Apollos became a very powerful witness for Christ."[203]

As previously mentioned, Apollos moved to the city of Corinth with a letter of recommendation from the Christians in Ephesus. He greatly helped those who through grace had believed and powerfully refuted the Jewish ideologues in public showing by Scripture that the Christ was Jesus, the true Messiah.[204] Paul's first epistle to the Corinthians (circa AD 55) mentions Apollos as an

---

[200] "Ephesus," *Wikipedia, last modified March 20, 2017, accessed April 3, 2017, https://en./Wikipedia/wiki/Ephesus.*

[201] Stanley, *Life Principles Bible, Acts 19:24,25.*

[202] Ibid. Acts 19:26

[203] Ibid. LIFE LESSONS, Acts 19:26, p.1290.

[204] Ibid. Acts18:27,28.

important figure from Corinth. He described his role, "I planted, Apollos watered, but God gave the growth."[205]

Paul 'picked-up where Apollos had left off in Ephesus' and explained the Gospel of faith, resurrection and eternal life. In a gathering, twelve men listening to Paul were baptized. After the ritual, Paul laid his hands on them and "the Holy Spirit came to them, and they began 'speaking in tongues.' The disbelievers and disobedient became hardened, deriding the teachings of *'The Way,'* so Paul left and taught and reasoned daily in the school of Tyrannus."[206] Some have suggested the school of Tyrannus was a private synagogue, but this seems unlikely in that the text seems to imply Paul reasoned in the only synagogue in Ephesus. Rather, it was probably a private school run by Tyrannus, and Paul was granted or perhaps rented the use of it each day.[207]

Another group with whom Paul dealt in Ephesus were the 'magicians and exorcists' who traveled through on occasion. One of the exorcists tried to use 'Jesus' as his power to heal, but the evil spirit who resided in the exorcized man told the exorcist, "I recognize Jesus, and know about Paul, but who are you?" The evil spirit departed, and the man who *had* the spirit leaped on the exorcists, so they fled from the house 'naked and wounded.' People in Ephesus heard about the disturbance and in turn more started coming to Paul and companions. "So, the word of the Lord was growing mightily and prevailing."[208]

After this, Paul was ready to leave and go through Macedonia and Archaia with his sights on Rome. Paul sent Timothy and *Eratus*

---

[205] Ibid. 1 Corinthians 3:5-6.

[206] Ibid. Acts 19:9.

[207] Thingspaulandluke.wordpress.com/2011-2013/04/07/13.

[208] Stanley, *Life Principles Bible, Acts 19:20.*

ahead but stayed in Ephesus for a while longer, and "about that time there occurred no small disturbance concerning *The Way*."[209]

The unique 'magnet' and major source of income and trade for the artisans in Ephesus was the great *Temple of Artemis*, the fertility goddess. Her shrine, four times larger than the Parthenon in Athens is considered one of the Seven Wonders of the Ancient World. It was revered throughout East Asia and the known world. The temple built of marble had an area in square footage larger than modern day football and soccer fields, and Diana's wooden statue stood in the very center.

Another major structure existed in the city – an immense amphitheater with a seating capacity of over twenty-five thousand spectators. Here and other similar amphitheaters featured fights between wild animals-and men, man-versus man, and gladiator combat. Ephesus had one of the largest cemeteries for dead gladiators in all of Asia Minor.

The city was a 'tourist attraction.' The city's commercial life and prosperity mainly depended on thousands of visitors visiting the temple and attending events in the stadium and theater.[210] The local artisans 'depended' on the income of tourists, especially those tourists buying miniature silver statues of Artemis.

When Paul began preaching doctrines that undermined the worship of Artemis (idol worship), the populace became alarmed, turning to rage as Paul's teachings disparaged the spirit of their livelihood and threatened the city's commerce and income (Paul

---

[209] Ibid. Acts 19:23.

[210] Bruce Dalton Barton, Philip W. Comfort, Kent Keller, Linda Chaffee Taylor and David R. Veerman, eds., *Life Application Bible Commentary (Carol Stream, IL: Tyndale House Publishers, 1996), p. xiv.*

always had a deep sense of dislike and outrage for any idols and idol worship).[211]

An artisan named 'Demetrius,' deemed to be the ringleader of the artisans, rose against Paul and his disciples. He said to all men and women in similar trades, "Men, you know that our prosperity depends upon this business. You see and hear that not only in Ephesus, but in almost all of Asia, this Paul has persuaded and turned away a considerable number of people, saying that gods made with hands are no gods *at all*. Not only is there danger that this trade of ours falls into disrepute, but also that the temple of the great goddess Artemis be regarded as worthless, and she, whom all of Asia and the world worship, will even be dethroned from her magnificence."[212]

This was quite a disturbance since it affected much of the city, and men rushed the disciples and dragged *Gaius and Aristarchus*, two of Paul's traveling companions from Macedonia into the theater. It was recommended to Paul 'not to go,' as much as he wanted to. There was much shouting and confusion, but *many* of the Ephesians didn't even know what the uproar was about, and it lasted about two hours.

A 'town clerk' came to the rescue and said, "Men of Ephesus, what man is there after all who does not know that the city of the Ephesians is guardian of the temple of the great Artemis and of the image which fell down from heaven? So, these are undeniable facts; you ought to keep calm and do nothing rash. For you have brought these men here who are neither robbers of temples nor blasphemers of our goddess. So then, if Demetrius and the craftsmen who are with him have a complaint against any man, the courts are in session and pro-consuls are available; let them bring charges against one another. If you want anything beyond

---

[211] Stanley, *Life Principles Bible, Acts 19:26,27.*
[212] Stanley, *Life Principles Bible, Acts 19:24–27.*

this, it shall be settled in the lawful assembly, for indeed we are in danger of being accused of a riot in connection with today's events, since there is no real cause for it, and in this connection, we will be unable to account for this disorderly gathering."[213]

With the 'temple incident' over, Paul left Ephesus under the competent care of elders, and 'commissioned Timothy' to minister there and wrote, "As I urged you upon my departure for Macedonia, remain on at Ephesus so that you may instruct certain men not to teach strange doctrine."[214]

The church in Ephesus truly was a remarkable church for Paul 'and the ages.' Scholars believe the apostle John wrote his letters and Gospel from Ephesus circa AD 85-90. After John's exile from Patmos ended, he returned to Ephesus for his final years. John also mentioned the churches of Asia to which Ephesus belonged in the Book of Revelations, "God commended the believers for their deeds, hard work, and perseverance.[215]

Paul decided to head to Macedonia and Greece. He traveled and met with assemblies formally established and stayed in Macedonia for three months; Paul heard 'a plot' against him was bubbling-up, so he left town, set sail with the intent of heading back to Syria, but again, changed his mind and traveled back through Macedonia.[216]

Paul sent his 'companions' ahead to Troas and Philippi and stayed in Troas three weeks spreading the word and exhorting to the gatherings to keep the faith and continue to 'walk in Christ's likeness.' On the final day in Troas, Paul spoke to a group meeting in a house until midnight. There was a young man, *Eurychus*, sitting in an upper window; he fell asleep, fell out the window, and died.

---

[213] Ibid. Acts 19:35-41.

[214] Ibid. 1 Timothy 1:3-5.

[215] Ibid. Revelation 1:4.

[216] Stanley, *Life Principles Bible, Acts 20:1-3.*

Paul embraced his body and said to him, "Do not be troubled, for his life is in him" (he walked away alive). They finished the dinner, and the next day, Paul was on the move again, this time back to Miletus. He only stayed a very short while as he decided a trip back to Jerusalem was within the time frame needed to return before the *Pentecost.* Not wanting to 'simply leave,' Paul called the elders from Ephesus and others to offer a memorable parting and farewell.[217]

At the gathering, Paul recapped all he, the apostles, and disciples had accomplished 'to the glory of God.' Paul told them he, "was on his way to Jerusalem, not knowing what will happen to me there," and reminded them, "as I testify to you this day that I am innocent of the blood of men. For I did not shrink from declaring to you the whole purpose of God." He also said ominously, "And now behold, I know that all of you among whom I went about preaching the kingdom, will no longer see my face."[218]

After Paul's farewell address, he added, "In everything I showed you that by working hard in this manner you must help the weak and remember the words of the Lord Jesus, that He Himself said, 'it is more blessed to give than to receive." When he had said these things, he knelt and prayed with all. And they *began* to weep aloud and embraced Paul, and repeatedly kissed him, grieving especially over the words which he had spoken, that 'they would not see his face again.' And they accompanied him to the ship."[219]

Paul, "not knowing what will happen to me there," was an un-beknown understatement. He sailed, landed at Tyre (in Judea). Staying there seven days, he met with disciples and related all that had been accomplished on his third mission, and finally left on foot for the coast destined for Jerusalem. *But*, not before many of

---

[217] Ibid. Acts 20:13-16.
[218] Ibid. Acts 20:25-27.
[219] Ibid. Acts 20:35-38.

the disciples "kept telling him through the Spirit not to set foot in Jerusalem."[220]

First and Second Corinthians

During Paul's third mission, he wrote two known letters to the Corinthians circa AD 55-57 written close in time with one another. There is speculation two other letters may exist but no records of the 'lost letters' have surfaced; one of the letters known as the 'letter of tears' was perhaps written between First and Second Corinthians.

The church in Corinth was experiencing major problems and issues, and the assembly wanted Paul's clarification on specific areas of doctrine. Paul and associates had realized building a 'coherent church' in Corinth would be a monumental task as the city was riddled with paganism, immorality, 'social climbing,' and was an area with a transient population. Paul also saw the advantages of living in such metropolitan cities, as the flow of 'new-possible' converts and non-believers seemed endless. By this time Paul had establish roughly twelve churches throughout East Asia, Macedonia and Greece.

Paul's letters addressed to Corinth provide an invaluable insight into the 'social world' of the converts, and the problems they encountered after embracing the new religion and faith - Christianity. They also provide an insight, more vividly than other New Testament documents, what it must have been like to attend and experience early Christian assemblies.

First Corinthians

In 1 Corinthians, Paul indicates his 'main opponents' were within the church, and followers were divided against one another *and* against Paul. 'A fact' the followers of the same church were taking

---

[220] Ibid. Acts 21:4.

one another to civil courts troubled Paul.[221] The faction of members who regarded their sexual activities as morally irrelevant felt they had 'already experienced a spiritual resurrection in their present existence,' and the most likely source of these false teachings was rooted in the Corinthians pagan background. The views of these opponents 'on power, prestige, and position' reflected values adopted from the Hellenistic world, particularly the emphasized Hellenistic views of speaking and communication. These opponents had the opinion that Paul's clear emphasis on the Gospel was "unimpressive and insignificant."[222]

Again, the emphasis of 1 Corinthians addresses the 'division and factors of the division' between church members.[223] The factions developed from loyalty to personalities rather to the person of Jesus Christ even depreciated the loyalty of those who professed allegiance to Him.

Apollos lived in Corinth now, and there were followers attracted by his 'eloquence.' Peter appealed to those who were more legalistic in attitude. The 'Christ party' viewed themselves as 'more spiritual than others.' Paul highlighted three factors contributing to division within the church:

- Misunderstanding the nature of the gospel, [224]

- Misunderstanding the nature of his ministry, [225]

- Human pride. [226]

---

[221] Stanley, *Life Principles Bible, 1 Corinthians 6:1.*

[222] Ibid. 1 Corinthians 10:10, 11:6.

[223] Ibid. 1 Corinthians

[224] Stanley, *Life Principles Bible, 1 Corinthians 2.8-10.*

[225] Ibid. 1 Corinthians 3:5-4:5.

[226] Ibid. 1 Corinthians 4:6-13.

Explaining the 'nature of the Gospel,' Paul pointed out the need to understand its content.[227] He insisted the central theme of the Gospel was 'the cross, Jesus Christ and the resurrection.' This message was a contradiction to Jews and Greeks who could not conceive of a 'crucified messiah.' "To Jews, Christ was a stumbling block as they envisioned a conquering king who would restore Israel, not a Savior who would forgive their sins. They could not accept Jesus was the 'fulfillment of the law, and only needed to have faith in Him to be saved.'"[228] The Greeks believed that a man who died as a lowly criminal "could not possibly be 'God incarnate and the Savior of the world.' Jesus bore no resemblance to their pantheon of mystical deities, so to believe in Jesus seemed foolish."[229]

The nature of the gospel demands a divine demonstration of power.[230] Paul offered a simple, unpretentious presentation of the truth when he ministered in Corinth, and the mighty results of his preaching demonstrated that God's power lay behind the message. He argued the nature of the Gospel demonstrated 'divine wisdom; the Gospel contains God's true wisdom'.[231] The wisdom of the Gospel is revealed by the Holy Spirit and produces believers of maturity. The performance of the Corinthians indicated they had not yet reached a proper level of maturity.

Some in the Corinthian church understood Paul's ministry as a competition. They viewed Paul and Apollos as competitors seeking to gain followers for themselves – *individually*. To overcome this concept, Paul pictured himself and Apollos as "servants"[232] and

---

[227] Ibid. 1 Corinthians 1:31.

[228] Ibid. Romans 9:31-33.

[229] Ibid. LIFE LESSONS, 1 Corinthians 1:23, p. 1329.

[230] Ibid. 1 Corinthians 2:1-5.

[231] Ibid. 1 Corinthians 2:2:5-3:4.

[232] Stanley, *Life Principles Bible, 1 Corinthians 3:5.*

"fellow workers" with God.[233] As a 'master builder,' Paul laid a spiritual foundation, saying the Corinthians must build on this foundation with great care.[234]

Rather than boasting of traits possessed by mere humans, the Corinthians should have realized that all of God's resources belong to them.[235] Only God can deliver an accurate evaluation of the contributions of human beings.

'Human pride' was another element contributing to disunity in the Corinthian church. Paul, acting as a pastor through this part of the letter reminded the Corinthians they have/had received 'all of their endowments from God.' It was sheer arrogance to boast of what they have. God has given it all to them as the 'free gift of grace.' For them to boast of their gifts from God would be like heirs boasting they had worked to earn the fortune of their inheritance.

Paul also addressed other 'moral problems' within the church, three in particular:

1. Incest,

2. Lawsuits among members and believers,[236]

3. Sexual Immorality.[237]

Another concern of the Corinthians centered around *marriage*.[238] Many in ancient times admired celibacy as a higher calling, and

---

[233] Ibid. 1 Corinthians 3:9.

[234] Ibid. 1 Corinthians 3:10.

[235] Ibid. 1 Corinthians 3:18-21.

[236] Ibid. 1 Corinthian 6:1-6.

[237] Ibid. 1 Corinthians 5:1-13, 6:18-20.

[238] Ibid. 1 Corinthians 7

Paul admitted celibacy as an acceptable option. He urged those married to stay married even if married to an unbeliever; those finding themselves in this situation might face troubles that would limit their Christian usefulness. Paul finally urged Christians to live content in the state in which God had placed them. To those single, he counseled the preference of the 'single state' over marriage. Marriage, however, was always an acceptable option. Widows were free to remarry, but should *only* to believers.

Paul urged the Corinthians to *'take care of their personal liberty.'*[239] Some in the church were invited to private meals where the meat from an idol-worshipping sacrifice was served, and asked Paul, 'What do we do?' His answer:

1. A Christian should never eat meat if the eating offends a weaker Christian,[240]

2. A believer should limit the right to eat meat if that freedom hinders the spread of the Gospel,

3. A Christian should never indulge in the freedom to eat meat if that action threatens the personal spiritual life of another individual.[241]

Paul believed everything ultimately "belongs to God,"[242] so if the message of consuming meat was sensitive to a believer, then the believer should simply abstain from eating it. Whatever they ate or drank must be done so for the glory of God without injuring even one of God's children.[243]

---

[239] Stanley, *Life Principles Bible, 1 Corinthians 8:1–11,*
[240] Ibid. 1 Corinthians 8:13.
[241] Ibid. 1 Corinthians 10:25-28.
[242] Ibid. 1 Corinthians 10:26.
[243] Ibid. 1 Corinthians 10:31,32.

Paul, over time learned the 'art of compromise.' Many of the Laws of Moses had been modified, some neglected, as they indicated works (how to get a person to heaven). His message was 'those who entered heaven, entered through a belief in Jesus Christ.'

Paul dealt with the issue of *incest* by writing more about the church's tolerance of the practice than about 'the man' who persisted in sexual relations with his father's wife, probably his stepmother. The church may have shown tolerance but even pagans did not accept such behavior, and he advised the church to expel the sinning member and "to cast him into the arena where Satan held sway and to cease all contact with the erring member."[244]

Paul joyfully maintained that the Christian life was an experience of freedom and liberty. Everything was permissible for him. To distinguish this statement from sexual license, Paul added two caveats:

1. He would do nothing that was not beneficial to his Christians life, and

2. He would not allow any habit to dominate him.

In the case of sexual immorality, Paul warned that this sin destroyed individual personality, and Christians are to view their bodies as a residence of the Spirit of God. Still other areas of disunity were *disorder in public worship* focusing on two issues – coverings for women and the Lord's Supper:

1. Corinthian women refused 'to cover their heads in worship' in defiance of the customs of the times.[245] Paul suggested the Christian women in Corinth 'cover their heads' to worship and Christian men worship without covering their heads.

---

[244] Ibid. 1 Corinthians 5:1, 5:11.
[245] Ibid. 1 Corinthians 11:3-7.

His intent may have been to follow accepted customs in Corinth, but some have suggested that 'long hair' on women satisfied the nature of the covering. Others suggested it was a 'veil;' the veil covered the hair, not the face, and was customarily worn by Greek women at the time.

One faction of the church saw the covering 'to show and indicate the submission of a woman to their husbands.' Others maintained it demonstrated *a woman's new authority as a Christian woman.*

Paul wanted women to respect their husbands but showing 'submission' did not seem to be his primary purpose for wanting women in Corinth to be veiled. Another idea as to his view on veiling was 'to show a sign of their *new authority to pray and worship in public.'*

2. The Corinthians celebrated the Lord's Supper as part of a fellowship meal for which each participant contributed food. The affluent brought plenty; the poor brought little, maybe nothing. The purpose was to share a 'communal meal.' The wealthy were privately eating to excess while the poor gazed upon the gluttony with empty stomachs.

   Corinthian Christians did not share fellowship during the celebration of the supper as they had been called to do. These conditions only established social factions and created disruptions among groups in the assembly from different social strata (rich versus the poor).

   The observance was to focus on *the cross, the death of Christ, and His resurrection.'* Paul advised those who could not avoid factionalism and gluttony as they participated to stay away from the public observances as some of these members were getting 'drunk and stuffing themselves.'

It was a visible division between the rich and poor. To Paul, the scandal was the Lord's Supper had become a stage for displaying the diversity between rich and poor instead of a time for expressing 'the unity of the body of Christ;' it had become an occasion for division. The Lord's Supper is a sacrament *to recognize Jesus Christ as the church, his crucifixion, and most importantly, his resurrection* and *was* the sole intent of the supper.

Apparently, the Corinthians never learned to do 'anything in moderation.' When they became aware that certain members had spiritual gifts, they prized the more spectacular gifts and 'talking in tongues' topped the list. The worship services could easily degenerate into an experience of frenzy and flamboyance with little moral substance. Paul's instructions were designed to correct these abuses of the Corinthians:

1. Paul emphasized the 'diversity of spiritual gifts.' Each believer had a special gift that should be used for the common good,

2. He emphasized 'the interdependence of all believers.' Within the Body of Christ, each gifted person made contributions, and then God blended all the elements into a single harmonious whole,

3. Paul taught the priority of love within Christian fellowship. One living in the 'Body of Christ' *displaced* envy, self-seeking, and pride. In the presence of God, Christians have no need for the revelation that speaking in tongues provided,

4. Paul emphasized the superiority of prophecy. Believers should seek prophecy because it promoted understanding and intelligent response (in Paul's time, reading the words of the prophets, and studying the Bible as a whole).

Two doctrines of Paul's teaching provide helpful direction for contemporary Christians. First, he emphasized that believers should seek the gifts that build up and edify other Christians rather than seek showy and exhibitionistic gifts. Second, he urged all believers to love one another.

There was the contingency in Corinth that denied the dead would rise. Such denial resulted *in rejecting* Christ's resurrection and robbed Christianity of its future hope. Those who died with 'no hope' for a future resurrection and eternal life were to be pitied. Paul attempted to correct the misunderstandings of this matter with the following points:

1. He *insisted on the reality of Christ's resurrection.* The resurrection was verified by post-resurrection appearances before groups of men and women (Pilate's wife claimed to have seen the resurrected Christ[246]). Paul emphasized the belief in the resurrection *is* the foundation of Christian faith.

2. Paul pointed to consequences of denying the experience of resurrection, saying that if Christ had not been raised, then our preaching is in vain, and Christians are still living with their sins, thus, denying the resurrection denigrates the very heart of Christianity.

3. He indicated the resurrection of Christ implied the resurrection of believers. The resurrection was the first step of the establishment of God's kingdom on earth and destruction of death.

4. He emphasized the resurrection of believers stating that 'hope of the future resurrection gives believers the courage to endure danger and hardship for the sake of Christ.'

---

[246] Frank Crane, "Letters of Pilate to Herod," *Lost Books of the Bible and the Forgotten Books of Eden (Newfoundland: World Bible Publishers, 1926), p. 276.*

5. He insisted believers would experience resurrection with an imperishable body suited for life in a world beyond. Since Christ's resurrection provides victory over death, Christians have an incentive to labor ceaselessly for the glory of God.

The last instructions concerned 'the collection for the saints;' those monetary gifts were to be sent to Jerusalem. At this juncture, Paul wanted to visit Corinth again, but instead sent Timothy. Timothy by this time had grown un-relentingly in 'his walk in Christ,' and Paul made the young man a valuable aide-de-camp during the second mission, and for the rest of his life.[247]

Second Corinthians

Second Corinthians suggests Paul wrote the letter soon after writing First Corinthians. Following a meeting with *Titus,* [248] and still in Macedonia, Paul wrote again to the church in Corinth. He wrote 2 Corinthians after receiving an enthusiastic report from Titus that the Corinthian friends had repented of their former hostility toward him and was happy that his letters had occasioned a positive time of repentance for the church. Titus's delivery of the letter reinforced the fact Paul wanted a relationship with the Corinthians and wanted to be part of their growing faith.

From Scripture, Paul's opponents appear to have re-infiltrated the churches 'from the outside.' These outsiders had a background in Judaism, but they were also heavily influenced by the Hellenistic world. In these opponents Paul confronted a Hellenistic Jewish movement who opposed him, but who were not as concerned with circumcision and Mosaic Laws as the Galatians.

---

[247] Lea and Black, *The New Testament: Its Background and Message (Nashville: B & H Publishing Group, 2003). Pp. 402–415.*
[248] Stanley, *Life Principles Bible, 2 Corinthians 7:6–16.*

Paul emphasized his desire to complete the *collection of money* being gathered for the poor Christian Gentiles and Christian Jews in Jerusalem. He also defended himself against determined detractors who represented a substantial threat. He wrote to warn the Corinthians against associating with professing believers who were living immoral lifestyles – the passages from 2 Corinthians 6:14-18. is clearly written to deal with separation from those who were unbelievers.

There is a fascinating scholarly argument as some believe that separate 'parts of 2 Corinthians' may have been written in short but chronologically ordered times as the first section addresses primarily the 'repentant majority of the church,' and the second section addresses the 'reactionary minority.' This may be due that during delays, Paul received additional information concerning Corinth indicating the church had fallen again into divisiveness *and* opposition to Paul. Paul's abrupt change in written tone in 2 Corinthians 10:1, might suggest the point at which he began his response to the new information. Paul nowhere indicates that he had received new information for writing chapters 10-13. He may have failed to mention the information because of 'personal attacks' against him.[249] Paul defended himself to whose behavior had changed because of the Corinthians changed attitudes.

Paul expressed in 1 Corinthians he planned to visit Corinth again, but changed his plans, but indeed, he finally made a trip in what he describes as the "painful visit."[250] He later returned to Ephesus, as perhaps one of his opponents suggested, 'that a leader (presumably Paul) who was so fickle lacked the necessary qualifications for the Christian ministry,' but Paul defended his ministry and *insisted his competence in ministry came for God.'* Paul based his ministry on the new covenant, and it was superior to that of Moses because the new covenant featured the ministry of the

---

[249] Ibid. 2 Corinthians 10:7-11, 11:1-6.
[250] Stanley, *Life Principles Bible, 2 Corinthians 2:1,2.*

Holy Spirit, produced righteousness, and provided permanence. Anyone who attacked Paul's ministry must reckon with its superior nature – **God!**[251]

Paul's change of verbal and written tone changes as one reads from chapters 8 – 9, and again in chapters 10 – 13. His words may have become more defensive and revealed a slight display in lack of confidence in a genuine response to the group he was addressing – I have a 'hard time' imagining Paul with a lack of confidence. Paul's 'change of tone' resulted as he was speaking to a hardened-rebellious segment of the church. This group either had ignored his appeals in 1 Corinthians ('the severe letter') or had begun to express additional forms of rebellion that came to Paul's attention after he wrote the first nine chapters. Paul referred to the charges against him as some accused him of showing timidity in face-to face contact but acting with excessive boldness in the safety of a letter. Paul insisted his attitude and behavior would be the same whether he was present or absent. 'Consistency of behavior' was Paul's practice.

Paul's opponents boasted of their ministerial accomplishments. They were claiming credit for the work Paul and the apostles had started. He insisted he would not boast of the work of another but would boast *only* of what Christ and God had done through him. Paul refused to commend himself for his work(s).[252]

Cunning, deceitful teachers were visiting Corinth and enticing Paul's followers away from their pure commitment to Christ. Paul was concerned some might accept the claims of the false apostles uncritically.[253]

Paul had 'never' accepted financial support from the Corinthians for his ministry and insisted he had never been a financial burden

---

[251] Ibid. 2 Corinthians 13:3,4.

[252] Ibid. 2 Corinthians 10:15-18.

[253] Ibid. 2 Corinthians 11:4,5.

to them. His opponents interpreted his financial independence as evidence of Paul's "lack of love for the Corinthians."[254] He assured his friends he had no interest in their money or material possessions. He gladly poured out his own possessions and personality for their benefit, and neither did he use Titus to exploit the Corinthians.[255] Paul insisted he would never change his practice as his refusal to accept funds prevented his enemies from boasting they worked on the same basis and spiritual plane as Paul – *which they did not!*[256]

Paul, again countered his opponents who boasted of their apostolic credentials as he preferred to delight in his 'weaknesses and hardships' rather than in his visionary experiences, and he did debate, and match, these opponents in every respect. The opponents, whom Paul named '*super-apostles,*' claimed to perform miracles and wonders in their ministries. Paul indicated these same signs *had marked* his ministry, in essence saying he was in no sense inferior to his attackers.

Paul wrote, and spoke to the Corinthians in strong tones, and terms, in order to strengthen them and build them up. He knew that jealousy, factions, and disorder had characterized the Corinthians. He 'spoke like a fool' so they might humble themselves and repent of their previous sins.[257]

Paul insisted that on a third visit he would not spare *any offenders* from his rebuke assuring the Corinthians he would speak with the power of Christ, and he challenged his readers to examine themselves and make certain they were following their faith and the Gospel. Paul's final exhortation urged the Corinthians to practice Christian unity; he closed with a Trinitarian benediction.

---

[254] Stanley, *Life Principles Bible, 2 Corinthians 5: 10-12.*
[255] Ibid. 2 Corinthians 12:14,15, 16-18.
[256] Ibid. 2 Corinthians 11: 14-16.
[257] Ibid. 2 Corinthians 12: 20,21.

After the letters written, his voyage back to Tyre after the third mission *and* 'apostles urging him not to return to Jerusalem,' Paul set-off for Caesarea, and stayed at the house of Philip the evangelist.[258] A prophet, Agabus came to Paul in Caesarea, and he too, told him 'there were Jews waiting to bind him, as they were aware of Paul's missions and teaching to Jews and Gentiles throughout Asia Minor and Greece.[259]' Paul, never one to fear a debate or fight, did not heed the warnings or back down – he headed to Jerusalem.[260]

Paul had a welcoming committee in Jerusalem including St. James and all the church elders. After greeting and meeting with them, he spoke of his mission(s) and how the Gentiles as well as many Jews had received the Word. Along with the 'welcoming party,' were Judaizers who were *not ecstatic* to see Paul again. His report 'concerning the Gentiles' who had believed included, "the Gentiles decided they should abstain from meat sacrificed to idols, from consuming the blood, from eating what is strangled, and from fornication."

Paul was advised to 'cleanse himself' in the temple along with four other young men. He entered the temple the next day, and the ritual lasted seven days.[261] Paul did return with monies 'for the collection' under the care of Timothy, Titus and the 'eyes of St. Luke.' Paul reframed from handling these funds. The next two years of Paul's life are full of 'trials and tribulation' and will be dealt with in detail in Chapter 13.

---

[258] Ibid. Acts 21:3,4.

[259] Ibid. Acts 21:10,11.

[260] Ibid. Acts 21:15.

[261] Stanley, *Life Principles Bible, Acts 21:23,24.*

Study Question for Chapter 10

1. Why was Ephesus an important church for Paul's missions.

2. What was interesting about Ephesus and surrounding area that appealed to Paul

3. What were inherent issues within the church assembly(s) in Corinth that Paul needed to address?

4. Where had many of these issued originated?

5. What 'spiritual gift' did the Corinthian church cherish the most? Why?

ST. PAUL AND THE COLLECTION

Paul mentioned his need to fund what he referred to as *The Collection* for the poor. He dealt with the collection in Epistles written during the second and third missions – Galatians, 1 & 2 Corinthians, and Romans. *The poor* refers to Christians in Jerusalem and was a term used in Judaism to reflect on the humble, godly, righteous citizens who were quite financially poor also known as the *pious poor.* The term was adopted as a self-designation of poor Jewish Christians.

The most extensive treatment of the collection is found in 2 Corinthians, and he received *the most* resistance from the Corinthians.[262] Paul began by challenging the Corinthians mentioning the example of the Macedonians who gave sacrificially.[263] Then he held up the ultimate example of self-giving . . . Jesus Christ, "who became poor that we might be rich."[264] [265]

Paul wrote that the basis for Christian giving to one another should be 'equality;' an example set with the equal portion of manna allotted to each Israelite in the wilderness. He then turned

---

[262] Stanley, *Life Principles Bible, 2 Corinthians 9:6-9.*

[263] Ibid. 2 Corinthians 8:1-5.

[264] Ibid. 2 Corinthians 8 & 9.

[265] Ibid. Philippians 2:6-11.

over details of the administration of the collection in Corinth to Titus and two other trusted disciples.

In the epistle to the Romans, Paul explained he was delaying his trip to Rome and possible mission to Spain in order to deliver the collection to Jerusalem first. The book of Romans was written during Paul's last visit in Corinth.

The Book of Acts, authored by St. Luke, is strangely silent about the collection. As extensively as Luke followed Paul's ministry and missions (and accompanied him), Luke mentions nothing concerning the collection. Paul always collected money for the poor Gentile and Jewish factions in Jerusalem as it was very much part of his ministry. Why Luke does not mention the collection, I do not know, nor can other resources give good reasons. Paul's own letters reveal that 'this third journey was undertaken to deliver the collection.'

The gathering of relief offerings likely had its origin in the church in Antioch as the areas around Judea had been continually hit hard by famines. Even during the Jerusalem Council, the Antioch offering provided the background to Galatians 2:10. In Antioch, Paul's Jewish-law free Gentile mission was endorsed by the leading apostles in Jerusalem. At the conclusion of his account of the Jerusalem meetings in the Galatians Epistle, Paul added that the apostles asked him to continue to remember the poor.[266]

The Fundamentals of Paul's Idea of the Collection

Paul did indeed start his collection process with the Galatians, but the first explicit directives about participating in the collection are found in Corinthians. Paul stated the purpose of the collection was to help the '*saints*;' he regularly called all Christians, 'saints,' meaning 'those who have been set apart in Jesus Christ.' Here, he

---

[266] Stanley, *Life Principles Bible, Galatians 2:10.*

had in mind the 'saints in Jerusalem.'[267]   Paul mentioned he had given directions to the Christians in Galatia as to the administration of the collection. This may not be a reference to the Epistle to the Galatians, but a reference to some other communication Paul had with the Christians in Galatia.

Galatians 2:10 establishes the principle of the collection and Paul's commitment to it ("the very thing I was eager to do"). This remains true whether one dates Galatians early or late. If one dates the Epistle to Paul's third mission, the reference may be 'a gentle reminder to the Galatians' of their own need to participate in the collection.

Paul's first 'directives' concerning their participation in the collection to the Corinthians, instructs them to "set aside money on the 'first day of the week.'" The first day of the week for Jews was Sunday, and this also seems to be an early reference to Sunday being a day for Gentile Christian assembly and giving.

Paul insisted that the offering was voluntary and should be only in proportion to the capacity of each person to contribute, and he wanted the church to administer the collection. At this point he seems to have left the matter entirely up to the Corinthians, and no representatives were sent to administrate the gift.

In 2 Corinthians there is more about the administration of the offering, and he grounded his appeal for the Corinthians' participation in three Christian principles of giving:

1. The first principle Paul mentions in light of the collection was that of 'Christian service.' Giving is a form of Christian ministry – a service and ministry.

---

[267] Ibid. 1 Corinthians 16:3, Romans 15:26.

2. The second principle was the Lord Jesus Himself set the pattern of giving for us all. He did not cling to his divine riches but became poor for our sake, so that we might become rich as his joint heirs. Paul may well have had Philippians 2:5-11 in mind.

3. The third principle is that of 'equality.' Christians should share with fellow Christians in need. Paul used the example of the God's allotment of 'equal manna' to the early Israelites while in the wilderness.

2 Corinthians 9 is devoted to establishing a theological basis for giving. Paul also founded Christian giving in "God's own righteousness;" a gracious God who maintains his covenantal love - God is "righteous" - providing amply for his own.

The Jews often used the word righteousness to refer to the practice of charity ('alms'). Paul saw the collection as an expression of thanksgiving to God for his *indescribable gift of Jesus Christ.*

Finally, Paul's 'overall' goals for the collection may be summed up in the following:

- Charity – the Jerusalem church had a constant need of all forms of help as famines during the era were numerous and severe.

- The eschatological basis – Paul's concept of his 'Gentile mission' was rooted in his conviction that Christ was the promised messiah. The Gentile mission was, in Jewish thought, an accomplishment to the messianic age.

- Christian unity – Throughout his ministry, Paul maintained a close relationship with the church in Jerusalem returning and visiting the Christians at the end of each mission. He went to Jerusalem voluntarily to secure Jewish-Christian recognition of his ministry to the Gentiles.[268] [269]

Paul seems to be the only apostle who placed *the collection* for the poor as one of the 'centerpieces of his missions.' He always expressed the fact that God provided everything saying that as believers we should do our part, 'no matter how little.' Paul believed that giving in God's name was very much an important part of Christianity.

Chapter 11 Study Questions

1. Where did the idea of 'the collection' originate, and whom was it intended to benefit?

2. Paul saw the collection as a service and ministry. How do you see it, and how do churches today support the many programs for the poor, needy and hungry? Name a few.

---

[268] James Dunn, *The Theology of St. Paul, p. 771.*
[269] John B. Polhill, *Paul and His Letters, pp. 306-312.*

Chapter 12

BACK TO JERUSALEM
"TRIALS AND TRIBULATIONS"

Paul had ended this third mission, returned to Judea, stayed in Caesarea with Philip of Caesarea and later walked to Jerusalem. Concern arose about his safety, and he was forewarned there were Judaizers who wanted him punished or executed. The Pharisees and Sadducees were lying in wait as they too, were not happy to see Paul's return.

Returning to Jerusalem, Paul was asked to have, and conceded to a 'ceremonial cleansing' in the temple. Ceremonial cleansing was a dimension of purity universal in religions seeking to move one away from 'disgust' (at one extreme) and to uplift one toward purity and divinity (at the opposite extreme), away from uncleanliness . . . to purity, away from deviant and immoral behavior within one's cultural context.[270] Paul was joined in this ceremonial cleansing by four young men who had become disciples and accompanied him back on the voyage from Greece. Jewish Christians harboring suspicions about Paul's laxity to the law suggested a plan to overcome their suspicions by asking him to pay the expenses of

---

[270] "Ritual Purification," *Wikipedia, Last modified April 2, 2017, accessed April 4, 2017, https://en.wikipedia.org/wiki/Ritual_purification.*

the young men who had taken a 'Nazarite vow;' a vow taken by those who voluntarily dedicate themselves *totally to God.*[271] Paul's actions would not involve him in compromise and would certify he lived according to the law. Further, it illustrated his principle of becoming 'all things to all men.'[272]

Paul went to the temple to begin his 'seven day'[273] ritual cleansing from any defilement. Jews from outside Jerusalem (perhaps from Ephesus) saw him in the temple and assumed he had 'defiled the temple' by allowing Gentiles to enter; an act punishable by death. Accusations were made against Paul, and a mob began to form. A Judaizer cried out, "Men of Israel, come to our aid! This is the man who reaches to all men everywhere against our people and the Law and this place; and besides he has even brought Greeks into the temple and had defiled the holy place."[274]

Accusations were made against Paul; the crowds that assembled were in an uproar and all of Jerusalem was in 'chaos and confusion.'[275] He was physically removed, dragged from the temple and beaten (again). Fortunately, Roman soldiers garrisoned at a fort at Antonia near the temple kept watch for such disturbances and quickly acted to quench the riot and rescue Paul. The Roman tribune sensing Paul was the focus of the trouble, arrested and bound him in two chains, and soldiers led him through the 'violent mob' back to the barracks where he could be questioned in quiet.

The crowd still not satisfied, followed the entourage of soldiers and Paul shouting, "Away with him!"[276] Paul asked the commander, Claudius Lysias, if he could have a word with him, and asked, "Do

---

[271] Stanley, *Life Principles Bible, Numbers 6:1-21.*

[272] Ibid. 1 Corinthians 9:19-22.

[273] Ibid. Acts 21:26,27.

[274] Stanley, *Life Principles Bible, Acts 21:28.*

[275] Ibid. Acts 21:30.

[276] Ibid. Acts 21:36.

you know Greek?" Apparently, an Egyptian had stirred the crowds to this degree of frenzy previously, and the commander wanted no trouble of the sorts. Paul told the commander he was a "Jew from Tarsus in Cilicia and asked if he could address the crowd when they arrived at the steps of the barracks." The commander quieted the crowd to "a hush" allowing Paul to speak and "he spoke in the Hebrew dialect."[277]

Paul speaking in Hebrew quieted the unruly mob more; he caught their attention. He gave an autobiographical account of himself from beginning -to end mentioning his birthplace Tarsus; he was a Jew and at one time a Zealot Pharisee initially persecuting those who were associated with '*the Way.*' He spoke of his Damascus road experience hearing and 'possibly seeing' Christ and being led into Damascus 'blind' after the encounter.' Paul knew after his encounter with Christ, he had been *appointed* to take his message to the Gentiles and mentioned "while in a temple, he fell into 'a trance and heard Christ say to him, Go! For I will send you far away to the Gentiles.'"[278]

This final statement set the unruly mob into a frenzy and raising their voices again said, "Away with such a fellow from the earth, for he should not be allowed to live!"[279] The commander at that point took Paul into the barracks and wondered why the local Jews were so adamant in their dislike of him. The commander wanted answers too and was determined to get to the bottom of why Paul was causing all this trouble. Paul was taken by a centurion, stretched-out, and was about to be 'scourged' (beaten, whipped -again) when he asked the centurion, "*Is it lawful for you to scourge a man who is a Roman citizen and un-condemned?*"[280]

---

[277] Ibid. Acts 21:40.

[278] Ibid. Acts 22:3-21.

[279] Ibid. Acts 22:21.

[280] Stanley, Life Principles Bible, Acts 22:25.

The centurion realizing the gravity of Paul's question went to the commander and told him, "What are you about to do? For this man is a Roman."[281] The commander came posthaste saying to Paul, "Tell me, are you a Roman?" The commander too was a Roman citizen but had bought his citizenship with money, and Paul said to him, "I was born a Roman citizen."

The commander realized he had made a 'major mistake' by even "placing Paul in chains" and wanted to end this incident – *fast*. The next day Paul was released from chains, and it was decided it was a 'Jewish matter,' and "the chief priests and all the Council were assembled; they brought Paul down and set him before them."[282]

Paul's presence before the Jewish Sanhedrin, Pharisees, and Sadducees did not go well. Apparently, they had already made up their minds. The scribes did somewhat come to Paul's defense, and again there followed a major uproar. Nothing was going to be settled, and the commander who accompanied Paul to the meeting decided to take Paul back to the barracks before he may have been killed.

Assurance in the Face of Danger

That night, Paul received a message from the Lord saying, *"Take courage; for as you have solemnly witnessed to My cause at Jerusalem, so you must witness at Rome also."*[283] A conspiracy was brewing against Paul, and there were more than 'forty' men who 'in secrecy' planned to kill him. Paul had a nephew, the son of 'his sister' who learned of the plot and had a centurion lead him to the commander with the information. He said, "The Jews have agreed to ask you to bring Paul down tomorrow to the Council as though they were going to inquire somewhat more thoroughly about him. 'So do

---

[281] Ibid. Acts 22:25,26.
[282] Ibid. Acts 22:29,30.
[283] Ibid. Acts 23: 1-11.

not listen to them, for more than forty of them are *lying in wait* for him who have bound themselves under a curse not to eat or drink until they slay him; and now they are ready and waiting for the promise from you.'"[284]

'In the third hour of the night,' the commander had Paul readied to be moved to Caesarea accompanied by horsemen, soldiers and spearmen; Paul was provided a horse also. He decided that Paul would be under better protection by *Felix the Governor*. A letter was sent along explaining the situation in Jerusalem and the commander wrote, "I found him (Paul) to be accused over questions about the Jewish Law, but under *no accusation* deserving death or imprisonment."[285]   When Paul arrived and was before Felix, he was asked 'where are you from?' He told Felix he was from Cilicia, and when Felix learned this, he said, "I will give you a hearing after your accusers arrive also," and then gave orders for Paul to be held in 'Herod's Praetorium.'[286]

Felix

Felix was the younger brother of the Greek freedman Marcus Antonius Pallas. Pallas served as a secretary of the treasury during the reign of Claudius. Felix was a Greek freedman (slave) either of Claudius, according to which theory Josephus Flavius calls him Claudius Felix, or of Claudius's mother, Antonia Minor, a daughter of Triumvir Mark Anthony to Octavia Minor and niece of Emperor Augustus. Tacitus further added, Pallas and Felix descended from the Greek kings of Arcadia. Felix became procurator by petition from his brother.

Felix's cruelty and licentiousness, coupled with his amenability to bribes, led to increased crime in Judea. The period of his rule

---

[284] Ibid. Acts 23 20-22.

[285] Stanley, *Life Principles Bible, Acts 23:29.*

[286] Ibid. Acts 23:33-35.

was marked by internal feuds and disturbances which he put down with severity.[287]

Felix was married three times (his second wife Drusilla of Judea, daughter of Herod Agrippa I and Cypros). Drusilla of Judea divorced Gaius Julius Azizus, King of Emesa to marry Felix. Their marriage had a sordid history as Felix had used a Cypriot magician to persuade Drusilla to leave her husband and marry Felix. The Judean Drusilla was one of two major figures dying in the eruption of Mount Vesuvius, the other, Pliny the Elder. After the eruption and death of Drusilla, Felix married a third time, but no information is available concerning his third wife.

Felix did have an initial examination into Paul's case and offered the Jews who accompanied Paul to Caesarea *a bribe* to curry favor with the Jews by offering to send and conduct another trial in Jerusalem. Paul balked at this dangerous concession and reminded Felix that he as *a Roman citizen could appeal for a trial to be conducted before Caesar* where a determination of a violation of any Roman law would be made.

The Jews who came to Caesarea to make a case against Paul brought their own attorney – *Tertullus*. They thanked Felix for hearing the case, said it would be brief, and laid out their evidence. "For we have found this man a *real pest* and a fellow who stirs up dissension among '*all the Jews throughout the world*,' and a '*ringleader*' of the sect of the Nazarenes. *AND* he even tried to desecrate the temple; and then we arrested him [We wanted to judge him according to our laws]. *BUT*, Lysias the commander came along, and with much violence took him out of our hands, ordering his accusers to come before you. By examining him

---

[287] "Antonius Felix," *Wikipedia, last modified March 14, 2017, accessed April 4, 2017, https://en.wikipedia.org/wiki/Antonius_Felix.*

yourself concerning all these matters you will be able to ascertain the things of which we accuse him."[288]

Then Felix nodded to Paul and allowed him to speak. Paul denied 'desecrating the temple, or the synagogue.' 'They cannot even prove *the charges* for which I am accused, and I did not incite riots. "According to *the Way* which they call a sect I do serve the God of our fathers, believing everything that is in accordance with the Law and that of the Prophets, having a hope in God, which these men cherish themselves, that there shall certainly be a resurrection of both the righteous and the wicked. In view of this, I also do my best to maintain always a blameless conscience *both* before God and before men."[289] Paul accused Jews 'from Asia' for starting all the violence and said they too, should be here with any accusations.

Felix had knowledge of *the Way,* and essentially decided to 'put off' the accusers telling them he wanted to see a full report from commander Lysias before deciding anything further. Paul was escorted back to prison and 'yet had some freedom' but was asked not to converse with friends or be ministered by them.[290]

Some days later Felix and his wife Drusilla, a Jewess came to see and talk with Paul. Paul talked about *righteousness, self-control and the judgment to come.* He apparently upset Felix, and finally Felix sent him away; "Go away for the present and when I find time I will summons you."[291] Felix did return on several occasions but with a plan to seek a bribe from Paul for his freedom, and this went on for two years while Paul remained in prison in Caesarea. Eventually, Felix was succeeded by *Porcius Festus,* and he left the entire matter in his hands.

---

[288] Stanley, *Life Principles Bible, Acts 24:5-8.*

[289] Ibid. Acts 24:12-16.

[290] Ibid. Acts 24:22,23.

[291] Ibid. Acts 24:25.

Festus went to Jerusalem to confer with the Jews who had brought charges against Paul. The Jews were trying to win a concession with Festus as they wanted Paul returned to Jerusalem (*at the same time,* setting an ambush to kill him on the way). Festus declined and said Paul would remain in Caesarea, and he too left Jerusalem back to Caesarea telling them to come and bring any proof of their accusations. After a day upon returning, Festus took his seat on the tribunal and ordered Paul to be brought before him and his accusers. The Jews reiterated the charges they had previously used before Felix, and again Paul said he had done 'nothing wrong;' "I have committed no offense either against the Law of the Jews or the temple or against Caesar."

Festus trying to appease the Jews asked Paul 'if he would return to Jerusalem and stand trial before him'. But Paul said, "I am standing before Caesar's tribunal, where I might be tried. I have done no wrong to the Jews, as you also very well know. If, then, I am a wrongdoer and have committed anything worthy of death, I do not refuse to die, but if one of these things is true of which these men accuse me, no one can hand me over. *I appeal to Caesar.*"[292] At that Festus conferred with his council and said to Paul, "You have appealed to Caesar, to Caesar you shall go."[293]

Paul Appears before Herod Agrippa II, Bernice and Festus

Paul had now been held prisoner under Felix for two years without being formally charged by the state (Rome). During the time, Felix had already begun the process of sending Paul to Rome; any Roman citizen had this right if he so wished to be tried by Caesar. Festus having become the new governor, expedited sending Paul to Rome. *Herod Agrippa II* and his wife, Bernice made a stopover in Caesarea days after Paul demanded his trial before Caesar.

---

[292] Stanley, *Life Principles Bible, Acts 25:10,11.*
[293] Ibid. Acts 25:12.

Herod Agrippa II officially name Marcus Julius Agrippa, at times simply called Agrippa, was the seventh and last king of the family Herod the Great, the *Herodians.* He was the son of the first better-known Herod Agrippa, the brother of Bernice, Mariamne, and Drusilla, Felix's second wife.

Agrippa II was educated at the court of emperor Claudius. At the time of his father's death he was only seventeen, thus Claudius kept him in Rome and sent Cuspius Fadus as procurator of the Roman province of Judea. While in Rome, Agrippa voiced his support for the Jews to the emperor Claudius and against the Samaritans and the procurator of the Judean province, Ventidius Camanus who had been suspected of causing much of the troubles in the region.

On the death of Herod of Chalcis in AD 48 AD his small kingdom of Chalcis was given to Herod Agrippa with the right of superintending the temple in Jerusalem and appointing its high priest. In AD 53, Herod Agrippa was appointed king by Claudius over the territories previously governed by Philip and Lysanias, surrendering Chalcis to his cousin, Aristobulus. Herod Agrippa celebrated by 'marrying off' his two sisters Mariamne and Drusilla. *Bernice was Agrippa's younger sister.*

After the death of her first husband, Bernice went to live with her brother Agrippa. Many scandalous rumors concerning their relationship circulated. Flavius Josephus, the Jewish historian, repeats the gossip Herod Agrippa "lived in an incestuous relationship with his sister Bernice."[294]

In AD 55 the emperor Nero added to his realm the cities of Tiberias and Taricheae in Galilee, and the Livias (Julias) with fourteen villages in close proximity to Peraea. Agrippa spent large

[294] William A.M. Whiston, trans., *The Works of Josephus (Peabody, MA: Hendrickson Publishers, 1987).*

sums of money in beautifying Jerusalem and other cities during his appointment.[295]

Festus related the 'perplexity' concerning the handling of Paul's case to Agrippa. Agrippa took interest in Paul's case and wanted the opportunity to hear Paul present his defense. That opportunity came the next day, and it was 'no small trial setting' as "prominent men in the city and commanders came at Agrippa's demand."[296] "So, on the next day when Agrippa came together with Bernice amid great pomp and entered the auditorium accompanied by commanders and the prominent men of the city at the command of Festus, *Paul was brought in.*[297]

> "Festus said, "King Agrippa, and all you gentlemen here present with us, you see this man about whom all the people of the Jews appealed to me, both at Jerusalem and here, loudly declaring that he ought not to live any longer."

> "But I found that he had committed nothing worthy of death; and since he himself appealed to the Emperor, I decided to send him."

> "Yet I have nothing definite about him to write to my lord. Therefore, I have brought him before you *all* and especially before you, King Agrippa, so that after the investigation has taken place, I may have something to write."

> "For it seems absurd to me in sending a prisoner, not to indicate also the charges against him." 'Festus *could not*

---

[295] "Herod Agrippa II," *Wikipedia, last modified January 31, 2017, accessed April 4, 2017, https://en.wikipedia.org/wiki/Herod_Agrippa_II.*
[296] Stanley, *Life Principles Bible, Acts 25:23.*
[297] Ibid. Acts 25:23.

see how Paul had violated the Jewish Law and hoped that Agrippa who knew the Jews well could help him formulate some kind of legal charge against him that would make sense to the Romans.'[298]

King Agrippa said to Paul, "You are permitted to speak for yourself." Then Paul stretched out his hand and *proceeded* to make his defense:

"In regard to all things of which I am accused by the Jews, I consider myself fortunate, King Agrippa, that I am about to make my defense before you today; especially because you are an *expert* in all customs and questions among the Jews; therefore I beg you to listen to me patiently."

"Since then, all Jews know of my manner of life from my youth up, which from the beginning was spent among my own nation and at Jerusalem."[299]

Paul goes on telling his life's story not leaving out anything from his time as being a zealot Pharisee, persecuting the people of *'the Way'* and his Damascus road encounter where he encountered the Christ; this is Paul's third time relaying his personal message about the Damascus road experience that can be found in the Book of Acts.[300]

While Paul was laying out his defense, Festus stepped up into his role (in a sense), 'master of ceremonies' and said in a loud voice:
"Paul, you are out of your mind! Your great learning is driving you mad."

---

[298] Stanley, *Life Principles Bible, Acts 25:24-27.*
[299] Ibid. Acts 26:3,4.
[300] Stanley, *Life Principles Bible, Acts 9:1-22; Acts 22: 1-18; Acts 26: 9-18.*

Paul replied, "I am not out of my mind, most excellent Festus, but I utter words of truth. For the king knows about these matters, and I speak to him also with confidence, since I am persuaded that none of these things escape his notice; for this has not been done in a corner."

Then Paul asked King Agrippa, "Do you believe the Prophets? I know that you do."

Agrippa *replied* to Paul, "In a short time, you will persuade me to become a Christian." And Paul said, "I wish to God, that whether in a short time or long time, not only you, but also all who hear me this day, might become such as I am, *except* for these chains."[301]

And so, ending the trial King Agrippa stood up, and asked to confer with Festus. "This man is not doing anything worthy of death or imprisonment," adding, "This man might have been set free if he had not appealed to Caesar."

Paul had earned his 'day in court.' He had proven himself beyond any reasonable doubt he was *not guilty* of anything the Judaizers had accused him, and serendipitously earned a 'free ride' to Rome – all expenses paid. Paul in his mind *never had a doubt* as God had told him repeatedly, he would make it to Rome.[302]

---

[301] Stanley, *Life Principles Bible, Acts 26: 24-29.*
[302] Ibid. Acts 19:21; Acts 32:11, 23:19; Acts 25:12; Acts 26:32

Chapter 12 Study Questions

1. Why was Paul apprehensive about returning to Jerusalem after the third mission?

2. From Scripture we find that Paul had a sister and nephew. What important role did his nephew play in Paul's life?

3. Where in Acts are the separate chapters and verses describing Paul's 'Damascus road experiences?'

4. How did Paul earn a 'free trip to Rome?'

5. Paul was a Roman citizen; how was this beneficial during this period of his life?

Chapter 13

THE BOOK OF ROMANS

The Epistle to the Romans, Apostle Paul's greatest work is placed first among his thirteen epistles in the New Testament. Some have called it his *Christian Manifesto*. While the four Gospels present the words and works of Jesus Christ, Romans explores *the significance of His sacrificial death*. Paul offers a systematic presentation of biblical doctrine.

Romans is a preeminent book when it comes to crucial topics such as salvation and faith; however, it is much more than a book of theology. It is also a practical exhortation about how to live in joyful obedience to God. *The Good News of Jesus Christ* is more than facts to be believed; it is an abundant life to be lived – a life of righteousness befitting the person "justified as a gift by God's grace through the redemption which is in Christ Jesus (Romans 3:4)."

Paul begins his letter by addressing the necessity of obeying the Lord with love and humility. He reminds the churches and synagogues in Rome that it is *through Jesus Christ that we receive eternal life as well as grace* for each circumstance a person may face. It is His salvation that sets us free from the power of sin. Until we come to a point where we acknowledge our need for a Savior, we cannot appreciate the gracious gift God has given people who can enjoy the gift of eternal salvation through faith in Jesus Christ who gives them the desire *and* the strength to obey the Lord.'[303]

Paul was on his way to Rome; but, during his third mission he penned the Book of Romans either prior to or just after he wrote the letters to the Corinthians. The letter was written circa AD 57. Paul's eastern missions were over; his face and eyes were focused on the West.

Paul was in Corinth when he wrote the letter to the Romans. Cenchrea was the seaport at Corinth on the Aegean Sea. "The reference to Cenchrea, the port in Corinth, the recommendation of Phoebe, a servant of the church and person about to depart for Rome was to carry the Roman letter were further indications of the apostle's whereabouts when he wrote the letter.

Phoebe was a first-century Christian woman mentioned by the apostle Paul in the letter to the Romans (Romans 16:1,2). A notable woman in her church of Cenchrea, she was trusted by Paul to deliver his letter to Rome. In writing of the church that was likely in her home, Paul refers to Phoebe as a deacon and patron of many, also known as a *'Prostatis.'* This is the only location in the New Testament where a woman is specifically referred to with these 'two distinctions.'

Paul introduces Phoebe as his emissary to the churches in Rome, and because the Roman believers may not have been acquainted with her, he provided her credentials. Phoebe's exceptional character noted by her status as a deacon and prostatis ('one highly esteemed "because of their work"') may be the primary reason Paul asked her to carry his letter to the Romans. By referring to Phoebe as a prostatis, Paul also solicits the attention and respect of the known

---

[303] Stanley, *Life Principles Bible, The Book of Romans Introduction, p. 1305.*

leaders in Rome's church which included women namely Prisca, Mary, Junia, Tryphena and Persis.[304]

Paul having finished his third mission was 'apprehensively' looking forward to his trip back to Judea. Unbeknown to him at this time, he would be spending two years in Caesarea in prison. Once the mission was to be completed, he could continue his dream to labor in his evangelical work. His choice of a future missionary journey was *Spain*, the oldest Roman colony in the West. A journey to Spain would afford him the opportunity to realize another lifelong ambition – to pass through and visit Rome and spend time with the Christian believers.

John B. Polhill in his book *Paul and His Letter* noted Paul had not met the Roman Christians (or Jews).   He wrote the letter "with considerable diplomacy." Even though the letter is lengthy, his comments appear to be general. Polhill recommends, as do many theologians (and, 'I'), "Paul's other Epistles need to be studied in conjunction with Romans. This may help have a better understanding on his specific views of major doctrines such as eschatology and Christology. Paul had planned all along to visit Rome, and his letter was designed to introduce him and prepare his way."[305]   There are several themes and purposes for writing throughout the letter that Paul wanted to introduce to the Roman Christians, and to all disciples during his lifetime and in the future – ***The Gospel***.

1. Paul wanted to share a spiritual gift emphasizing mutual encouragement. He was not just coming for a visit; his desire was to preach and teach the Gospel in Rome. Paul knew the Roman church had come into existence without

[304] "Phoebe (biblical figure), *Wikipedia, last modified March 12, 2017 accessed April 3, 2017, https://en.wikipedia.org/wiki/Phoebe_(Christina_woman).*

[305] John B, Polhill, *Paul and His Letters (Nashville: B & H Publishing Group, 1999), p. 278.*

the authoritative leadership of an apostle to the Lord; Paul was offering his services to add validity to their existence by instructing them in the faith through his epistle.

2. The very first chapter, verses 16-17 sets the theme for the entire epistle; Paul was not ashamed of the Gospel as he believed it represented the very power of God Himself. The power of God and the righteousness of God are virtually synonymous; both relate to God's salvation of believers. Paul stated this salvation was "first for the Jew, then for the Gentile." This is a subtheme of the entire epistle – God's *impartiality* in dealing with both Jews and Gentiles. Paul was emphatic in his claim to be the *Apostle to the Gentiles*, and Rome was the capital of the Gentile world.

3. Paul wanted to deposit a compendium of theological truth. The capital city of the empire was the natural place for him to do so; Paul was apprehensive about his immediate trip to Jerusalem. Perhaps the letter to the Romans would be his *final opportunity to draft a theology* of the Christian faith in a written, changeless form as he believed it.

4. As Dr. Adam, W. Miller states, "He bequeaths to them in the form of the Epistle, the Gospel that he would preach to them, should he be permitted to reach there, and if not, they have his letter to read and refer to again and again." Paul certainly fulfilled these purposes. The Epistle has proven to be the epitome of evangelical Christianity.

Structural Facets of the Book of Romans

One interesting facet 'in *source books*' used in this study of Romans, *is* many authors and scholars break their works on Paul's Romans into two books: Chapters 1 – 8 and Chapters 9 – 16. Footnotes in this text may refer to other Epistles of Paul to help clarify the points and theology he presents in Romans. It is important to pay close attention to the Bible and read verses when 'noted.'

Perhaps it is wise to conclude that Romans does not contain a *'single theme'* but discusses a wide range of Christological concepts. Justification by faith, union with Christ, and the history of salvation certainly appear in the text of Romans. We're to see a clear explanation of Paul's Gospel and an appeal for unity (Romans 14:1-15:13).

The Reformers focused on *justification by faith* as the theme of the Epistle. Others identified Paul's main emphasis as the experience of union with Christ discussed in chapters 6 – 8; others discovered the focal theme in the history of salvation narrated in chapters 9 – 11.

Paul wrote salvation was "first for the Jew, then for the Gentile." This is *a subtheme for the entire epistle: God's impartiality in dealing with both Jew and Gentile.*[306] For millennia, the Jews were known as God's chosen people from Abraham on. The birth of Jesus (the Messiah), his teachings, theology, and ideology changed everything (something many Jews could not or would not wrap their hands-or heads around). The Torah for the Jews had been replaced by the *Torah of Christ* for both Jew and Gentile.

Paul states, *'there is only one means of being accepted by a righteous God; that being through faith in God's own provision of Christ's atoning death.'* Living in and believing in Christ is the only divine means of being accepted by a righteous God, and any other attempt one may make is futile and will fail.[307]

In Romans 1:20, "God has another witness to Himself besides the primeval revelation; a witness than cannot be corrupted by

---

[306] Lea and Black, *The New Testament, 14-16.*
[307] Kroll, *The Book of Romans, p.16.*

man – the witness of *Creation;* [308] *God's witness is universal.* Paul, even if in a limited sense, believed human beings could learn from nature and the truth of God's eternal power it represents. He knew God as *omnipotent, omniscience, and eternal,* saying that no person can fully understand or comprehend the nature of God. Paul knew that those who were accepting Jesus Christ as the Son of God and trying to comprehend the idea of the "one true God" needed to be careful of "overthinking the concept of God," and read and comprehend what he is presenting in his Epistle, as follows:

- Paul warned against a willful rejection of God's revelation of Himself. This is known as *atheism and is a glorification of human intellect.* There are many who think and believe their way is the correct way to some form of (ultimately false) salvation. Look at the New Age movement, astrology and similar beliefs rampant in our society. A question should be aimed at those who wander in thought and from Christian theology; *'Is your life full of peace and joy, or just more questions?'*

- Paul addressed idolatry in Romans 1:22-25. Two beliefs stand out in a study of Paul:

1. His love for and belief in the *One True God, and Jesus Christ,*

2. His hatred of idolatry, worshipping false gods, and making use of symbols.

Coveting false gods, idols, and belief systems leads to a form of "enslavement." J. V. McGee asked, "How much longer will God

---

[308] John Phillips, *Exploring Romans (Grand Rapids, MI: Kregel Publications, 2002), p.26,*

be patient with us."[309]   Paul sensed many would-be believers had turned from God - to Satan, 'the author of the lie and father of idolatry.' As much as Paul hated idolatry, it had to bother him when the Corinthians were returning to pagan gods and idol worship. He sensed they were losing their original love-of and trust in his Gospel of Jesus Christ. He may have thought of the Corinthian church and the issues it was facing as Romans was written very close in time when Paul was in Corinth.

- In the first verses of Romans 2, Paul addresses self-righteousness in general. It seems to be particularly appropriate to the Jewish sense of moral "rightness" over the pagan world.

- God judges all people *impartially* on a basis of what they are and their conduct, *not their privilege*. It is the *sole criterion* of God's judgment. In some of Paul's new Christian assemblies, there were factions of people who believed they were closer to God than others because of their perceived value in the church (they were wealthy or had the ability to speak in tongues).

God's righteousness comes without discrimination *to all*, Gentile and Jew. Paul wanted to show the Jews had no edge over the Gentiles by merely possessing the law.   God will accept those who fulfill the demands of the law whether they are ignorant of the law (Gentiles). There is however a larger issue, whereas the law has a place in making *one aware of sin, it cannot make one right with God.*

---

[309] J. Vernon McGee, *Thru The Bible Commentary Series: The Epistles – Romans Chapters 1-8 (Nashville, TN: Thomas Nelson Publishing, 1991), p.42.*

- Chapter 3 is the center of Paul's argument in Romans. What we as humans cannot do for ourselves, God has done for us in Jesus Christ. Paul's basic interpretation of God is *'He is right and just.'* God alone establishes all standards of rightness. Human sin is not right; it is unrighteous, intolerable to a righteous God. Sin thus renders us unacceptable to God. *We, of ourselves, cannot deal adequately with sin.*

This is Paul's thesis in the first three chapters of Romans. Now, Paul shows that God had in Jesus Christ *provided the means for removal of our sin and our establishment as being righteous and acceptable in His eyes.* God making us righteous through Christ is called in English theological terminology-*"justification."* Another way to interpret the term *justification or to justify* in legal terminology is "to be pardoned." The new status *"in righteousness"* or in being right with God comes through *"faith in Jesus Christ."*[310] Paul deals with the theological term of *justification* in the following chapters of Romans:

- Chapter 4 enters the areas of Paul's basic theological beliefs. Believers are made right with God, thus *"justified"* solely through God's grace. *'Grace refers to God's free, unmerited gift.'* This gracious gift of God is further described as *redemption.*

  The removal of sin is described in terms of God's *"sacrifice to atonement."* Paul emphasized that Christ is the means of obtaining God's forgiveness of our sins.[311] "We are atoned, made one," made acceptable to God through the blood of Christ. *"Blood"* is

---

[310] Stanley, *Life Principles Bible, Romans 3:22.*
[311] Ibid. Romans 4:25.

Pauline shorthand for the death of Christ, but Paul understood Christ's death as *"a sacrifice."*[312]

- Chapters 5-8 expands more into Paul's theology and may make one look into other Pauline Epistles for better reasoning and understanding. By cross-referencing verses from the Pauline Epistles and passages in Romans, a reader may get a clearer idea of what Paul had in mind. After one accepts Christ, Paul believes the person becomes a *"new being in Christ."*[313] This was important to Paul as he believed *the Holy Spirit moved into a person's being* when he or she accepted *'Christ as Savior'* thereby making the person more Christlike.

Chapters 5-8 are considered *transitional chapters*. From the beginning of Chapter 5 the text enumerates the benefits of the new life in Christ; *a discussion* Paul returns to and treats more fully in Chapter 8. No portion of Romans states more clearly the "forensic" (legal) nature of our acceptance in Christ than Chapters 5-8.

God accepts us regardless of our sinfulness. The righteousness God grants us *is not a legal fiction*. God grants us His Spirit to enable us to grow into the full measure of His standards, His righteousness. These four chapters and their inferences can be cross-referenced in many of Paul's letters.[314]

Some feel Paul is a 'little hard on the Torah.' He opened himself up to charges that he was *antinomian* (a person who maintains Christians are freed from the moral law by virtue of grace as set-forth in the Gospel), and he completely disparaged the law of God. In Chapter 8 Paul illustrates the real basis of Christian life, "not

---

[312] Kroll, *The Book of Romans, p.61.*

[313] Stanley, *Life Principles Bible, Romans 8:11.*

[314] Polhill, *Paul and His Letters, p. 290.*

law, **but Spirit**." This is the language of reconciliation, a concept more fully explained in passages from Ephesians.[315]

Paul's focus was on humanity's *corporate solidarity with Adam*; Adam represents all humanity. Adam's sin began all human sinfulness. *The only way to eternal life is to share in the resurrection life of Jesus Christ.* The text expresses all humans inevitably share in Adam's sin. On the other hand, each person is ultimately-*individually* responsible. Each one has to stop and reflect on his or her actions or thoughts and determine individually whether they constitute a sin or not. If the action or thought is not deemed to be correct according to God's law and the Spirit of Christ, only the individual can make that assumption and correct the act or thought so *to live in this life, like Christ.*

Paul also connected sin with law. He argued that sin is more fully accountable where law is present because law establishes the rules and boundaries. Paul granted that sin was in the world between the time of Adam and Moses (when the law came into existence), because death reigned over *all* during that time. The conclusion is simple: "From Adam on, all humanity, those with and without the law have been bound up in the sin of Adam."[316]

Fortunately, Paul explains there are two humanities: humanity in Adam and *the humanity in Christ* – the latter being the *second Adam.* Through the disobedience of Adam came condemnation and death. *Through obedience to Christ comes righteousness, eternal life, and full acceptance by God.*

Paul clearly states the universal membership of all humanity in the sinful 'first Adam's existence.' Contrasting Christ with Adam, he speaks of Christ's obedience as bringing an eternal and spiritual

---

[315] Stanley, *Life Principles Bible, Ephesians 2:8-10*

[316] Irving L. Brittle Jr., *It's Not Rocket Science – The Theology of St. Paul* (Bloomfield, IN: iUniverse, 201, p. 34.

life for all people. This all-inclusiveness is, however, conditional at best. Christ's atoning work is the remedy for the salvation of all, none-the-less *it must be appropriated in faith by 'each individual.'*

Paul was convinced of the ultimate triumph of the work of Christ. No matter how bad the sinfulness of the 'first Adam (and all humanity),' *it cannot eclipse the grace of Christ which abounds in life eternal. Eternal life with Christ should be the primary goal of believers.* "The how" are the spiritual and theological mechanics of faith in Christ and is a '*lifelong journey; believers walk with Jesus Christ.*' Christ was sent by God to remove all sin from a believer. Forensically, *the sinner has been eternally pardoned – in the past, in the present and in the future.*

- The theme of Romans 6:10 – 7:6 is the "new life in Christ as death to sin." Paul's insistence that salvation is *achieved by grace* and *not by works* raises an ethical question: *why not sin in order that grace might abound?* Paul emphatically rejected this idea using three analogies to establish that "right living" is a necessary accompaniment to the "justified life."

1. The first analogy is *Christian baptism.* "The new life in Christ as death to sin"[317] is Paul's fullest treatment of baptism. He describes it as "dying and rising with Christ."

   Scholars still debate *where* Paul derived his ideas concerning baptism. It is unlikely he derived his ideas about baptism from Greek mysteries as some have maintained. More likely it developed along with his closely related ideas of 'the new creation in Christ,' and Christ as the 'second Adam.'

   Paul was not presenting a theology of baptism. Indeed, immersion in ritual cleansing baths, and *mikvut,*

---

[317] Stanley, *Life Principles Bible, Romans 8:2.*

had been part of Judaism for millennia. Paul used the picture of baptism to portray how the Christian buries the old life by participating in Christ's death, and then, *is raised to new life.* It was more than a picture for Paul. Believers do not die in baptismal waters; *they die with Christ in his actual death on the cross.*

2. Paul's second analogy developed in Romans 6:15-23, *is slavery.* One can either be a slave to sin or a slave to God's righteousness – it is strictly either, or. *One cannot be a slave to two masters at one time.*

   Paul developed a paradox. He maintained that when we are slaves to sin, we really are not free to do right. Now that we are *in Christ,* we are slaves to righteousness and are not free to sin. *Christians are <u>truly most free when they enslave themselves to Christ.</u>*

3. Paul's third analogy is perhaps the most difficult to grasp. Paul's main point is *'marriage establishes legal bonds.'* When *death* ends a marriage, the legal encumbrances are dissolved.

   As Christians we have died to sin and are now free from sin and free to marry righteousness. When making the former analogies, Paul wanted to make the point, *being,* the Christian life is *a life of righteousness* in the moral as well as the legal sense. *Not only have we been accepted as right by God, but we must also grow in rightness.*

His third analogy becomes somewhat confusing when Paul introduces the law into the mix. *Paul believed that sin and the law are the source of immorality.* As Christians we have died to sin; we are now free from sin and free to marry righteousness. When making the former analogies, Paul wanted to make the point, *being, the Christian life is a life of righteousness in the moral and legal sense.* Not only have we been accepted as right by God, also we must *grow in rightness.*

The third analogy becomes somewhat confused when Paul introduces the law into the picture. Paul believed that sin, the law and death are bound closely. When we die to sin, *we also die to the law-centered way of living.* Romans 6:6 is the key. For Christians, *the Spirit of Christ, not the law, is the source of immortality.* Paul returned to this theme in Chapter 8, but first he treated the pressing question of the law and its purposes.

- For the Jew, the law (as presented in the Torah) represents God's covenant with Israel. It accomplishes God's gracious election of Israel as His people, and Paul is very critical of the law *up to this point.*

- Paul argues strenuously that one cannot be saved through observing just the provisions of the law. He connects the laws with sin and death. For the Jewish Christians of Rome, as for the Jews in general, Paul's stance must have presented issues and problems.

If the law is an expression of God's covenant; was God reneging on His promise to Israel? Paul had already begun to discuss this problem in Romans 3:1-10. It had two main aspects:

1. The nature and the purpose of the law,

2. The abiding validity of God's election of Israel.

Paul's treatment of the law falls in two main sections:

- The first section deals with the law's role in human sinfulness. Paul emphatically denied that the law is itself, sinful. To the contrary, the law represents *God's will* and, as such, is *"holy, righteous, and good."*[318]

Humanity's problem is not God's law, but sin, 'rebellion against the law.' Law, however, contributes to sin; first it reveals sin as sin. It sets the standards and makes one aware when one transgresses.

Law serves as a catalyst for sin; the prohibitions increase the desire. Finally, *the law establishes responsibility*. The law sets God's norm, thus making someone accountable for transgressing the law.

In Romans 7:7-11, the verses are written in the first person singular. Whom did Paul intend with this "I" (probably not himself)? Paul never lived without the law. The passage may draw from the story of Adam and Eve's temptation in paradise.[319]

- The second part of Paul's treatment deals with the inadequacy of the law to deal with sin.[320] Paul continues in the "I" style, but this time in the present rather than in the past.

"The Law did not produce death"[321] according to Paul. Sin was the culprit. The law merely brought sin into the open, exposing it, as it is real. There follows the classic description of the "I" who is divided between 'willing and doing,' the "fleshy" individual who knows what is right *but cannot do what is right* because sin perverts

---

[318] Stanley, *Life Principles Bible, Romans 7:12.*

[319] Stanley, *Life Principles Bible, Romans 7:7–11.*

[320] Ibid. Romans 7:13-25.

[321] Ibid. Romans 7:6.

his or her best intentions. Throughout this section, Paul speaks in strong dualistic terms of life and death, sin and righteousness, flesh and Spirit.

Unlike the Gnostics, Paul's dualism was ethical, not metaphysical. He did not view 'the flesh' as inherently evil. The evil body is not the physical body; it is the body yielded to sin that is evil. The same body can be righteous and good when yielded to God's Spirit. But Paul's main point is that this sinful self cannot do what is right. The law can inform the conscience. It can produce the "willing," but it cannot produce the "doing." The presence of sin renders it ineffective.

Who is the "I" who experienced this ethical frustration of willing, but not 'doing.'" Was Paul referring to his own pre-Christian experience of wrestling with the Torah? Not likely! The pre-Christian Paul seems to have viewed himself as "faultless" with respect to following the law.[322] Of course, the Christian Paul, looking back on his former life may have seen it all quite differently. Was Paul perhaps referring to Jews in general and to the failure of their law-centered life?

- There is little evidence between "willing and doing" the law. Paul may have been referring to Christians; Christians alone would be fully aware of the pull of their life between God's standards and their failure to measure up. Romans 7:25 seems to point in this direction in Paul's life; short of the resurrection we are not yet perfected and are still a slave to sin's law, but in *our innermost self* we belong not to sin but to God. We are "in Christ," no longer to the 'first Adam.'

In the end, one may not really have to choose between the various alternatives. Paul may have been expressing the experience of everyone, Jew or Gentile, Christian or non-Christian who seeks

---

[322] Ibid. Philippians 3:6.

to lead a life that measures up to God's standards. Such persons are doomed to failure when left to the own resources, their own desiring and willing. Sin is too powerful a force. Only one thing can deliver us from the bondage to sin and its inevitable consequences of death. *"Thanks be to God."*[323]

Romans Chapter 8

Chapter 8 concludes Paul's treatment of the new life in Christ. The main emphasis of the chapter is *"assurance through the Spirit."* The Holy Spirit is the believer's assurance that times of tribulations in this life, and a perfect life will one day surely come for the one who trusts in God. Chapter 8 can be divided in four themes:

1. Romans 8:8-11 deals with the questions raised in Chapter 7. *What the law could not do, the Spirit has accomplished for us, giving us freedom from sin and death*. God provided the cure for sin Himself by sending His Son into sin's own territory ("in the likeness of a sinful man"[324]) as a sacrifice for sin. Not only did this secure the forgiveness of our sins, but also furnished us with the power to deal with sin through the gift of the Spirit.

    Verse 8:4 affirms the "righteous requirements" of the law. In its moral aspects, the law really does embody God's standards. The Spirit enables us to live by those standards.

    Romans 8: 5-11 returns to the theme of Romans 6: 1- 7:6. 'The death of the Christian to 'the old sinful nature' is described in terms of *'the indwelling Spirit.'* Manifestation of the Spirit is a necessary mark of the

---

[323] Stanley, *Life Principles Bible, 2 Corinthians 9:15.*
[324] Ibid. Romans 8:3.

Christian.[325] True, the Christian still lives in a sinful world and mortal body, but the Spirit provides the power to cope with sin's pull and gives assurances of the immortal resurrected life to come.[326]

2. Second, through the Spirit comes certainty we are God's children.[327] In our present life we appear to be no different from the rest of humanity, but in fact, *we are God's children,* joint heirs of God's kingdom through our relationship to God's true Son, Jesus Christ.

    The Spirit gives us inner assurance of our new status of being heirs with Christ leading us to affirm *God as Abba, our heavenly Father.* Even though we are heirs of God's kingdom, suffering often marks our lot in this life.

3. The third section deals with this tension between our future glory and the suffering of this present life. Through the Spirit comes assurance of the perfect redemption that is to come.[328] Our present existence is not perfect. Even the created order is witness to the present imperfection and eagerly awaits the future when the kingdom of God will come to power, and God's true children will come into their inheritance.[329] Here, Paul shares the prophetic vision of a new heaven and new earth, and the realization that somehow, even the non-human creation shares in the human tragedy. Modern eschatological studies have demonstrated for us how very true this is. Of course, it is not only nature that waits.

---

[325] Ibid. Romans 8:9.

[326] Ibid. Romans 8:10-11.

[327] Stanley, *Life Principles Bible, Romans 8:12-17.*

[328] Ibid. Romans 8:18.

[329] Ibid. Romans 8:12-22.

4. Christians "groan" awaiting the full redemption to come, the exchange of the mortal body for the glorious resurrected body.[330] The Spirit undergirds our hope, but it remains a hope, not a present reality.[331] Verse 26 and 27 show how the Spirit undergirds our lives in our present imperfections and inadequacy. *We don't even know how to pray*, but the Spirit intercedes for us, speaking beyond human capacity on God's level, in God's manner, and in accordance with God's purpose.

Verses 28-30 conclude the discussion of the Spirit's assurances in our lives' imperfections by affirming the absolute steadfastness of God's eternal plans. God will surely bring to completion the fullness of the coming glory for which the Spirit is our present guarantee. Verse 28, a debated text, does not express naïve optimism. In context it means *'in spite of all the imperfections, suffering, and adversity in this life, God's plans for his children will prevail* as we *work toward the ultimate good in the full realization of God's kingdom.'*

Verses 29-30 make, basically, the same point but in more *predestinarian* language. Paul uses a chain of past-tense verbs to emphasize the certainty of our salvation by pointing to the various stages of God working in our lives. He *foreknew* us; knew us before eternity. He *predestined* us for salvation before all time. We did not choose Him; *He called us.* He *justified* us, accepting us as His own without any merit on our part. He *glorified* us making us joint heirs with Christ in the life to come. Glorification is part of the future, but Paul was so certain of it, he

---

[330] Ibid. Romans 8 23-25.

[331] Ibid. Romans 8 23-25.

spoke in the past tense as if it were an accomplished reality.

Paul's *predestinarian* language is always a way of expressing God's grace. It emphasizes that our relationship with God does not depend on our own doing but on God's, God's will and God's plan for our life. Our assurances rest in the purpose of God. *Paul never eliminates human responsibility.* Somehow the divine sovereignty and human response *intertwine in the mystery of divine election.*

Romans Chapter 8 ends with a hymn of praise of God's triumphant love in Christ.[332] It serves as a fitting conclusion to 'Paul's entire message' from Romans 1:16, and on. Verses 31-34 develop the theme of non-condemnation through a series of rhetorical questions. God has chosen us in His beloved Son whom He gave up for our salvation. *"If God has chosen us, who can possibly condemn us?" Our relationship with God is secure.*[333]

Verses 35-39 (Chapter 8) developed the theme "no separation" of Christ from those He loves. No early calamities, or supraterrestrial[334] forces; absolutely nothing can separate us from God's love in Jesus Christ.

In the preview of these chapters on Romans, there are authors, biblical scholars, academics who feel the Book of Romans could easily been written as two books. The first half deals with and outlines Paul's theology. The second half would address Israel and God's plan of salvation (Romans 9-11:36). Most theologians see Romans as a "thematic book" (body of topics for study or discussion

---

[332] Stanley, *Life Principles Bible, Romans 8: 31-39.*

[333] Ibid. Romans 8:31.

[334] "supraterrestrial," not in any dictionary. It may mean *"a force beyond any known force."*

book of) to be studied by church members, church assemblies and believers.

There was a time when Romans Chapters 9-11 was considered peripheral to the main arguments found within the first-eight chapters. Currently, others feel these chapters are at the center of the epistle, and Paul's concern for Israel is behind every portion of the letter.

Most current interests in Romans 9-11 grows out of the dialogue between Jews and Christians and the issue of anti-Semitism. Thus, many recent analyses see Paul as directing himself more against Gentiles than Jews or as emphasizing throughout these chapters, the inclusion of Jews.

These chapters address the continuing validity of the old covenant,[335] between God and Israel apart from the "new covenant in Christ." That Paul was concerned with Gentiles feeling superior to the Jews is evident in Chapter 11. It is difficult to avoid the conclusion that Paul's main concern was the 'failure of his Jewish contemporaries to respond to the Gospel.'

Romans Chapters 12:1-15:3 contains "practical advice for Christian living." Paul often concluded his epistles with such hortatory sections of scripture. This form of ethical instruction was common with the other teachers in Paul's day, and the instructions were usually general in nature.

Christ presented Himself as a *sacrifice for us*. The proper and logical response to *this divine act of grace* is to sacrifice ourselves in sacred service to Christ. Christians are to live in genuine empathy and harmony with one another, meaning *'putting aside all pride and arrogance.'*

---

[335] Stanley, *Life Principles Bible, Deuteronomy 32:43.*

Paul dealt with the issue of *'not repaying evil with evil.'* Echoing Jesus's teaching concerning loving one's enemies, he quoted Proverbs 25:21, 22 to establish the principle of nonretaliation as means to winning one's antagonists over implying that the desire for vengeance can be destructive. When believers seek to repay evil with evil, they are dragged down to the evil's level and always lose. One's persecutors might be within the Christian community, but more than likely however, Paul had his eye on 'outsiders.' Paul broadened his focus beyond the Christian community in the latter chapters which deal with Christian relationships to "the state."[336] Paul took a conservative stance pointing out the secular rulers are established by God.

The purpose of government is 'to preserve the good and punish wrong.' Christians, as such must be subjects of government, otherwise they will incur God's wrath and suffer judgment.[337] Christians will violate their own consciences by transgressing what God has ordained. Paul tells Christians they should render respect to officials, pay their taxes and fulfill other civil obligations.

Some have suggested Paul was addressing a 'viable' situation in Rome as there was evidence of unrest over heavy tax burdens in Rome at the time. Paul felt Christians needed to be 'especially' careful not to appear seditious (Paul's judgment 'was on target' considering what happened to Roman Christians living under Nero less than a decade after he wrote Romans).

Paul, of course had in mind a government that functioned as 'an instrument of God.' He does not address a situation where the government has become 'demonic' and opposes God (can we relate this to our modern era?!?), as St. John's experience had to face

---

336 David S. Dockery, ed. *Concise Bible Commentary (Nashville TN: B & H Publishing, 2010), p. 550.*

337 Stanley, *Life Principles Bible, Romans 13:5-7.*

in the time of Revelation. St. John's experience with the Roman government differed radically from Paul's.

Paul goes on to relate the subject of *loving one's neighbor*. In this context, the word *'neighbor'* reaches beyond the Christian community and includes outsiders. Jesus summarized the law in terms of *"love for God and love for one's neighbor."*[338] Paul noted 'love can work no evil against one's fellow neighbor and is why it embraces all provisions of the law.' This section in Romans is a key passage in the current debate over Paul's understanding of the law. Paul recognizes the abiding validity of the provisions of the law while at the same time, invoking a higher principle of fulfilling the law.

Romans 13:11-14 establishes the eschatological basis for all Christian relationships. *"Christians should live in constant expectation of Christ's return."* This eschatological hope provides Paul a basis for the present Christian life. Each day is to be lived soberly, expectantly. Waiting in the light of the new day (the Lord's return), Christians should put behind past deeds of darkness.[339] Clothed in Christ, one removes the encumbrances of worldly ways. The best commentary on this passage is Ephesians 5:3-18, which shares most of its themes found in Romans.[340]

The Roman church to which Paul was writing was not different from the church assemblies he founded, or those that were in place throughout Asia Minor and Greece. Members of the Roman church had divided ideas, in this case over 'food and drink.' There were those 'who felt superior' to one group (as those found in the Corinthian church), and those seemingly trod upon who felt the other group "had no scruples" in dealing with Jesus Christ. Paul condemned both groups for their judgmental attitude reminding

---

[338] Ibid. Matthew 22:37-40.

[339] Ibid. Ephesians 5:8-13,

[340] Ibid. Ephesians 5:3-18.

them *the true basis for such matters was their relationship with Jesus Christ*[341] and their relationship to one another. Both groups stood on equal ground under the Lordship of Christ. Rather than judge one another they needed to worry more about how they would fare in God's judgment. What *'counts'* for the Christian is not indifferent matters like food and drink but important ideals and goals as righteousness, peace, joy in the Spirit, and building one another up.[342]

In Romans 15:1-13, Paul concludes his treatment of the divisions within the church in Rome by urging the Romans Jews and Gentile Christians to live in harmony following the example of Christ. In Romans 15:7-13 it becomes apparent that the divisions in the church were between Jewish and Gentile believers. Paul reminds the Gentiles that Christ came to the Jews to confirm the promises to the patriarchs. He reminds Jews that Christ came as a minister to the Gentiles and supports both these affirmations with scripture.[343] [344] [345] [346]

Many scholars question the reason for Romans 16 as it is composed almost entirely of a series of greetings to Roman friends whom Paul had met elsewhere. Some insist that Romans 16 may have been omitted from Paul's original letter, but no textual evidence supports this claim. It's more appropriate to view the extensive greeting in Romans 16 as an effort by Paul to establish friendships and credibility with Christians in a city he had not visited.[347]

---

[341] All 'Italiics' in 'Chapter 13, The Book of Romans' Added by the Author.

[342] Stanley, *Life Principles Bible, Romans 14:1-15-3.*

[343] Ibid. Psalms 18:49.

[344] Ibid. Deuteronomy 32:43.

[345] Ibid. Psalms 117:1.

[346] Ibid. Isaiah 11:10.

[347] Lea and Black, *The New Testament, p. 393.*

In the final verses of Romans Paul sends greeting from his co-workers as done in many epistles. Paul mentions *Tertius,* a disciple who may have had the opportunity to be Paul's 'amanuensis' (secretary or scribe). Paul also sends greeting on behalf of Gaius with whom he stayed in Corinth and on behalf of Erastus, the 'director of public works.'

These prominent men likely had 'acquaintances of means' in Rome. One of Paul's concerns was to secure material support in the Roman church for 'his hopeful Spanish mission,' and the protocol of including many greetings may have been in large part to address that concern.[348] [349] [350]

Paul had a good insight into human psychology. He needed friends (many) to help support his future mission(s). Familiarity breeds friendships and trust; those mentioned in the closing were likely appreciative of Paul's recognition of them and may have been more supportive as a result. It was very important for Paul to 'lay as much groundwork' as possible with the Roman church whether he personally knew many of the people who would see the letter, or not. Paul wanted to take a mission to Spain, and from experience he knew in order to do so, he needed backing and resources.

Study Questions for Chapter 13

1. Who was Phoebe, and why was she so important to the sending of the Epistle (Romans) to Rome?

---

[348] Wright, *Paul for Everyone, Part 1, Chapters 1-8.*

[349] John Phillips, The John Phillips Commentary Series, *Exploring Romans (Grand Rapids, MI: Kregel Publications, 2002), pp. 257-258.*

[350] John B. Polhill, *Paul and His Letters (Nashville, TN: B & H Publishing, 1999), p.300.*

2. Why do theologians, authors and researchers consider the Book of Romans to be the 'Christian Manifesto' and Gospel of Jesus Christ?

3. Why would Paul extend special greeting to many in Rome whom he didn't know and people of "means and importance?"

Chapter 14

A PERILOUS SEA VOYAGE TO ROME

Paul had been in custody and imprisoned for over two years after his arrival from the third mission. Arrested in the Spring of AD 57, he was eventually transferred to Caesarea and imprisoned there for two years. Having made his appeal to Caesar, he was transferred by a grain cargo ship bound for Rome in the fall of AD 59. He was shipwrecked along with his personal bodyguard, *Julius,* a centurion, delaying his arrival in Rome until the Spring of AD 60. St. Luke accompanied Paul on 'the perilous sea voyage' and wrote the story of the sea voyage down to the minutest of details.

Paul remained under 'house arrest' after his arrival in Rome while awaiting his appearance before Nero. During these two years Paul wrote four letters known as the "Captivity Epistles: Ephesians, Philippians, Colossians and Philemon." There is strong speculation that Colossians and Philemon may have be written while Paul *'may'* have been imprisoned in Ephesus for some unknown reason. Neither Paul nor St. Luke mentions anything in the Book of Acts about this possibility.

Paul, along with 276 passengers (including crew, prisoners and others) was boarded on-and sailed from a seaport on the Aegean

144

Sea in an Adramyttium grain ship.[351]   St. Luke was one of the passengers along with the Thessalonian Aristarchus, a member of the collection ensemble who had gone with Paul to Jerusalem. Julius, a centurion of the 'Augustan cohort' and bodyguard sailed with Paul; Julius had intended to take a short voyage to Troas, and then head-off to Rome by land.

One of the first ports of call was the community of Sidon where Paul visited the Christian community; Julius's trust of Paul played a major role in the overall narrative and voyage, and Julius let Paul's visit go unsupervised. On the following day the ship set sail 'under the shelter of Cyprus because the winds were contrary.'[352] During the autumn of the year, the winds blew predominantly westerly. As a result the ship could not sail on open seas but had to hug the coastlines. "They sailed along the coastline of Cilicia and Pamphylia and docked at another port at Myra in Lycia. Here, Julius found an Alexandrian-grain (presumably rice) ship sailing for Italy, and he put us aboard it."[353]

Because of predominantly westerly winds, the ship had to take a mostly serpentine route which added to the length of the journey. The ship rounded Crete from southern Asia Minor and set anchor in a small port named *Fair Haven*. Fair Haven had too small a harbor for the ship to spend winter. From mid-September through the winter, the Mediterranean Sea is treacherous. An immediate decision had to be made to sail on to Phoenix. Under favorable conditions, this leg of the trip would have taken only a few hours.

The owner of the ship, his pilot, Julius, and even Paul were called to make the decision to sail, or not. Of the four, Paul was the only one to suggest they stay anchored in Fair Haven the best

---

[351] A. N. Wilson, *The Mind of the Apostle (New York: W.W. Norton, 1998), p. 246.*

[352] Stanley, *Life Principles Bible, Acts 27:4.*

[353] Stanley, *Life Principles Bible, Acts 27:4,5.*

they could. Paul was overruled, and the voyage continued. "When a moderate south wind came up, supposing that they had attained their purpose, they weighed anchor and began sailing along Crete, close inshore."[354]

When the ship set sail, the weather seemed to be cooperating, but then a 'great storm from the north ensued. Luke described the winds as those of a typhoon.' The ship 'floundered' in the choppy sea and ended up blowing twenty- three miles south to the small island of Cauda (modern Gozzo). Protected from the winds on the lee side (the sheltered side) of the island, the crew initiated emergency plans to keep the ship afloat. The crew began to jettison cargo, the ships tackle and rigging and lowered the sails. The pilot and crew's main concern was the ship could be blown south onto the sandbars and shoals off the North African coast known as the *Syrtis* – known in those times as "a graveyard for ships." These dangerous sandy shoals were located off the northern coast of Libya on the southern side of the Mediterranean.

The storm raged-on for days, and the crew continually jettisoned more of the ship's rigging and tackle. Eventually, the crew gave up 'all hope of being saved.' But Paul admonished all as he had a *vision from God* that the ship and crew would make it to their destination. Unfortunately, the crew, the captain, and Julius could not comprehend Paul's message and continued adrift for fourteen days.

The crew and prisoners had nothing to eat for days, and it was ironic that the cargo holes were loaded with grains (possibly, consumable rice). The 'looming concern' regarding the cargo was if it got wet, it would expand (cook rice and watch it expand) and possibly split the hull. The cargo hatches were not opened; if opened, 'this action could possibly sink the ship!'

---

[354] Ibid. Acts 27:13.

Pretty much all hope was gone as the storm raged. But Paul rose and addressed his fellow shipmates. He told them he had a vision and word from God that his trip to Rome would be completed, and he would appear before Caesar. He then offered a different sort of message, not a warning but a word of hope and encouragement. "For this very night an angel of God to whom I belong and whom I serve stood before me, saying, "Do not be afraid Paul; God has granted you all those who are sailing with you. Therefore, keep up your courage, men, for I believe God that it will turn out exactly as I have been told. *But we must run aground* on a certain island."[355]

Paul had first conceived of his Roman witness in Ephesus.[356] In a previous vision God had assured him such a thing would happen.[357] Now for a final time he was given the same assurance, and because God would deliver Paul for his trial in Rome, he would *deliver all* on board the ship. The safety of the crew and all who accompanied Paul was now tied to Paul, his vision, and his purpose-driven life.

At midnight of the fourteenth day the crew heard breakers on rocks off Point Koura at the northeastern corner of Malta. The crew aware of the sound of breakers on rocks decided to drop four anchors from the stern to hold the ship in place until morning light. They dropped the anchors from the stern rather than the bow so the ship would head toward the shore when they attempted to 'beach the ship.' The crew assumed correctly their situation was particularly dangerous and perilous. They started to lower the lifeboat telling those on board they wanted to drop anchors from the bow.

Paul saw through the ruse and pointed the crew's actions out to Julius; the centurion heeded Paul's advice. He had his men cut the ropes to the lifeboat and set it adrift. The action seemed extreme

---

[355] Stanley, *Life Principles Bible, Acts 27:23-26.*

[356] Ibid. Acts 19:21

[357] Ibid. Acts 23:11.

as the lifeboat could have been useful later in evacuating the ship if need be. Perhaps, Julius felt the crew would try to lower it again when he may have not been looking. In any event, he realized the soundness of Paul's advice. Without the expertise of the mariners, it would be difficult for the passengers to make it ashore safely.

Again, Paul rose to address the crew and passengers. He strongly urged all to partake of food for strength. He explained to his fellow voyagers they need the food for their salvation (the New International Bible version uses the word *survival*). After eating their fill, the crew jettisoned the grain in order to lighten the ship for beaching. The *'salvation'* word-family occurs seven times in the journey narrative. In all instances it refers to the physical deliverance of the crew and passengers after the shipwreck. For Christians however, it is a word with more spiritual overtones. One may wonder 'did St. Luke use it with a certain symbolic meaning?'

The same applies to Paul's words of blessings over the food in Acts 27:35, 36. The familiar pattern of taking bread, giving thanks, and breaking the bread is the pattern in The New Testament accounts of the Lord's Supper.[358] It is the pattern of blessing that Jesus followed by feeding of five thousand,[359] and the pattern Jesus followed when dining with the original apostles.[360] It was the customary Jewish mode of giving thanks before a meal. Still, it is so much associated with Jesus that one wonders if the meal on the ship did not impart some special assistance of the Lord's presence for the Christians and crew aboard.

The night, finally ended, and the crew did try to beach the ship. On the way toward the shore, the ship hit a clay-based sandbar, stern first. With the pounding seas, the ship broke apart.[361] 'It

---

[358] Stanley, *Life Principles Bible, Luke 22:19, 1 Corinthians 11:23,24.*

[359] Ibid. Luke 9:16.

[360] Ibid. Luke 22:19; 24:30.

[361] F. F. Bruce, *Paul: Apostle of the Heart Set Free, p. 373.*

was every man for himself,' and that included the prisoners. This presented a dilemma for the Roman guards, including Julius; if a prisoner were to escape under any circumstance, it meant a 'death penalty' for the guard involved. The guards deciding to avoid the death penalty planned to kill all the prisoners. Again Julius intervened and rescued the prisoners. Everyone did reach shore safely and had Julius and Paul to thank. Paul's blessings and his God's answered prayers were factors in that *all survived.*

Without compasses or other navigational devices, the crew had no clue where they had landed. Fortunately for all on the voyage, they landed on the Island of Malta where they spent the winter- approximately three months. The island was under the administration of a Roman procurator likely by the name of Publius.[362] Speaking the language seemed to be a challenge as the native islanders spoke a form of Punic which dated back to a time when the Phoenicians occupied the island. In any event, the Maltese native population was very hospitable to which St. Luke mentions in scripture.[363]

The Maltese natives had a story of a former shipwrecked stranger who was bitten by a 'viper' and died. During his stay Paul was also bitten by a viper but lived. The Maltese natives thought of Paul as a god, but he quickly dispelled that notion telling them he was one "protected by God," both from the snake bite and the shipwreck.[364]

Paul and St. Luke healed many while on Malta, including healing Publius's father who was sick with dysentery and fever.[365] After Paul had healed the father, word spread, and whole neighborhoods brought their sick to Paul and St. Luke.[366] Luke does not mention

---

[362] F.F. Bruce, *Paul: Apostle of the Heart Set Free, p. 247.*

[363] Stanley, *Life Principles Bible, Acts 28:1,2.*

[364] Ibid. Acts 28:3-6.

[365] Wilson, *The Mind of the Apostle, p.247.*

[366] Stanley, *Life Principles Bible, Mark 1:30-34.*

Paul's witnessing to the native Maltese people, but wherever Paul traveled his acts of healing and witnessing went with him. Maltese Christian tradition naturally insists that such was the case; Paul is given credit for bringing Christianity to their island.

In February once the weather had improved, Paul, Luke, Julius, and the crew set sail on an Alexandrian ship that had wintered in Malta. The ship followed a normal route from Malta via Syracuse at the southeastern tip of Sicily, and then on to Rhegium at the 'tip of the boot' of Italy.

There was a stop-over in Rhegium awaiting favorable winds. When a southerly wind arose, they set sail through the Straits of Messina northward to Puteoli, making the 210 mile journey in a single day. Puteoli (modern Puzzuoli) was the ship's designation. In Paul's day, Puteoli was the main port for the large grain ships sailing from Egypt. Disembarking at Puteoli, Paul found a Christian community with whom Julius allowed Paul to stay for seven days. It is unknown when or how Christianity first arrived in Puteoli, but it may have been by means of former Jewish-Christian travelers witnessing in a local synagogue. After the week in Puteoli, *Paul's entourage set out on foot for Rome.* The route covered 130 miles and would take five days. The route went by the Via Campana, north to Capua, where it merged with the Appian Way.

On the Appian Way, Paul's entourage stopped at a market town named for the forum of Appius located forty-three miles south of Rome. There, they were met by a group of Christians who had come from Rome to greet them. Word of Paul's arrival had preceded the group soon after they docked in Puteoli. Paul's Epistle to the Romans had the obvious effect of introducing him to the Christians in Rome. This separate group from Rome was so eager to meet Paul they traveled two days south to intercept him.

After Paul's troupe traveled another ten miles, a second assembly of Roman Christians met him at the way station of *Three Taverns*. From Three Taverns the large assembly traveled together, north. Paul was elated his prayers had been answered, but he was still in chains.

Despite his not being the apostle who had brought the Gospel initially to the Romans, despite the ignominy of his chains, he was warmly received by the Roman Christians. With the arrival of the Roman Christians to welcome the apostle, Paul surely felt his intentions to visit the Roman congregations were already complete; Paul, at last, arrived in Rome. Paul was granted even more freedom as a prisoner (unchained) in Rome than he had experienced under Felix back in Caesarea. He was allowed to 'live alone, have visitors and with only one soldier to guard him versus the normal 'two guards.' Paul's lodgings were private and were provided for "at his own expense."[367]

Chapter 14 Study Questions

1. Who was Julius, and what segments of the voyage does he play a part in?

2. There are authors and scholars who believe Paul was a 'seer, a man of visions.' What were three 'visions' Paul shared with all on board during his sea voyage, and why were they important? (Choose any of the three)

3. St. Luke accompanied Paul on the voyage. Why was this *very good* while they were shipwrecked on Malta?

4. Did Paul's Epistle to the Romans precede him? Why might you believe it did?

---

[367] Polhill, *Paul and His Letters, pp. 383-389.*

Chapter 15

PAUL'S WITNESS IN ROME

The end of Chapter 28 in the Book of Acts addresses Paul's time in Rome. Nothing is ever mentioned concerning his impending appearance before Caesar, or if he ever gained any audience with Caesar. There are credible reasons why Paul may never have stood before Caesar. We must remember Paul had two visions and messages from God indicating the he would travel to Rome to spread the Gospel; at this point whether his stood before Nero was secondary. Given Paul is the Apostle to the Gentiles, we expect to read the account of his witness to the Gentiles in Rome, but instead we are given a more accurate picture of his witness to the Jewish community in Rome. The Acts narrative is one for which St. Luke may have been preparing us for all along. It consists of three primary scenes, as follows:

- Paul's initial conversation with the Jewish leadership,[368]

- Paul's witness to a larger group of Jewish citizens, [369]

- Paul's witness in his rented quarters to "all who came to him."[370]

---

[368] Stanley, *Life Principles Bible, Acts 28:17-22.*

[369] Ibid. Acts 28:23-28.

[370] Ibid. Acts 28:30,31.

The Jewish community in Rome when Paul arrived in Rome was large at about fifty thousand; most were poor. These communities were spread over the entire city. How the Jews were treated as people varied from Roman leader–to Roman leader.

Julius Caesar and Augustus Caesar stayed out of the lives, trades, and businesses of the Jews. Julius and Augustus Caesar believed the Jews had the right to hold their own religious gatherings and collect the monies for their Jerusalem collection, and exempted them from military service.

There were times when rights *were* restricted as was the case under Tiberius in AD 19 who consigned four thousand young Jewish men to serve in the military in Sardinia. During the reign of Tiberius many Jews were compelled to leave the city as a result of four Jewish con-artists bilking a Roman patrician matron out of a considerable sum of money. Approximately forty years later, Emperor Claudius expelled the Jews from Rome after 'uprisings' in the Jewish communities (Priscilla and Aquila who were living in Rome at this time were expelled and eventually found a home in Corinth).

Paul had arrived in Rome and was asking for an audience with Caesar to defend himself regarding the charges leveled against him by a small group of Jews in Palestine. Many in the Jewish population were delighted to have Paul in Rome; others were apprehensive.

Paul first met with Jewish elders and rabbis from a local synagogue at his residence. He wanted to assure them he was not in Rome to cause trouble, and wanted to curry their favor for his impending audience with Caesar. Paul assured them he had been found innocent in Caesarea of any wrongdoing and claimed that his current custody was unwarranted. Paul also informed and assured the elders he had lived faithfully to the Jewish tenets and laws.

Paul concluded by centering on the real issue that brought him to Rome – *the hope of Israel.* It was the main issue that separated Paul from many Jews – *his belief in the resurrection of Jesus was the fulfillment of the Jewish messianic hope and fulfillment of scripture by the Prophets.* All along, this had been the central underlying issue that led the Jews in Palestine to bring Paul to trial(s).

Surprisingly, the Roman Jewish leaders responded by saying "they had heard nothing about Paul, nor received any letters from Judea concerning him."[371] Perhaps the winter hiatus and sea voyage had prevented any communication from Jerusalem. These leaders may *not* have had a particularly close relationship with the Jews in Jerusalem, or possibly, they were being diplomatic with Paul but were eager to learn more of what he had to say; Paul was equally eager to share his witness.

Paul's witness to the Jews in Antioch, Syria[372] and his witness to the Jews in Rome[373] form the frame around his entire ministry as presented in the Book of Acts. The Antioch event stands at the beginning of his ministry, and Rome stands at the opposite end; they are strikingly similar. Both consisted of two stages of witness; an initial limited witness followed by subsequent witnessing to larger groups.

In both, Paul's message proved to be divisive with some believing and others disbelieving. In both, there came a time when Paul turned his attention and ministry to the Gentiles. In both, the turning is explained in light of a scripture from Isaiah. At Antioch the book of the Prophet Isaiah[374] serves as the scriptural basis for Paul's proclaiming 'the light of Christ' to the Gentiles.[375] In Rome,

---

[371] Stanley, *Life Principles Bible, Acts 28:21, 22.*

[372] Ibid. Acts 13:14-50.

[373] Ibid. Acts 28:17-28.

[374] Stanley, *Life Principles Bible, Isaiah 49:6.*

[375] Ibid. Acts 13:47

Isaiah 6:9-10 was cited to establish the failure of many Jews to respond to the Gospel.. This scripture also served as Paul's reason for turning to the Gentiles.[376]

This was the well-established pattern of Paul's ministry, to begin with the Jews and then turn to the Gentiles; a pattern repeated consistently throughout the Book of Acts. There was no reason to think things would be different in Rome.

The failure of Israel to respond to the Gospel was a fact that Paul experienced throughout his ministry; something he addressed with anguish in the Book of Romans.[377] In Romans, Paul did not abandon his 'hope for Israel's conversion.' There was no reason to believe he did so with the Jews in Rome.

A larger group of Jews came to listen to Paul on a second occasion; the size only limited by the confines of Paul's rented quarters. Paul preached all day seeking to convince the group by citing scripture from the books of the laws of Moses, and scripture written by Prophets claiming that Jesus Christ was the promised Messiah. Again, this was Paul's 'modus operandi' of approaching the Jews with the Gospel hopefully persuading them on the basis of scripture. The response to Paul's witness to the Roman Jews also followed a familiar pattern; many did not believe, but there was a smaller group who did.

With 'a house figuratively divided,' the Jews began to leave Paul's quarters, but not before he had an opportunity to relate one final message to his visitors. He again quoted Isaiah 6:9-10 where the Prophet speaks of God's word:

"They had ears that should hear, eyes that should see, and hearts that should be able to feel and to will. But,

---

[376] Ibid. Acts 28:26-28.
[377] Ibid. Romans 9-11.

their hearts were hardened and could not feel, their ears were dull and could not hear, their eyes open and could not see."

Otherwise, they would have turned and received God's deliverance.

Paul had seen the same things happen to the Jews of his generation. In fact, Isaiah 6:9-10 was the text that Jesus cited when referring to the failure of the Jews to respond to His teachings of His parables in the Gospels of Matthew and Mark.[378] Paul's words to the Roman Jews were not words of rejection *but of a challenge.* Unfortunately, some Jews did not respond as found in Chapter 11 Romans. The Book of Acts ends somewhat on a tragic note; in Paul's lifetime he did not see many of his fellow Jewish people embrace the Gospel as he so 'longed for them to do.'

St. Luke abruptly ends the Book of Acts and does not continue writing about the 'two-year' custody of Paul in Rome. We can surely assume Paul continued witnessing to those who came to him. Customarily, after two years in custody, if a person did not come to trial or before Caesar, he or she was released and 'free.'

Both, Festus and Agrippa 'noted Paul would have been freed after his trials in Caesarea if he had not appealed to Caesar.' Between the final discourse of these two men, there was mention of paperwork, or notes that had to be addressed to Rome regarding Paul's trials, their judgments on his dispensation, and the fact that both said 'they would not have brought any charges against Paul.'[379] Those correspondences may have made it to Caesar (Nero) before, or during Paul's two-year house arrest; Nero may have felt *the matter was immaterial* or simply a Jewish matter and not offered an audience.

---

[378] Stanley, *Life Principles Bible, Matthew 13:14, 15: Mark 4:12.*
[379] Ibid. Acts 25:25-27.

In *'Paul: Apostle of the Heart Set Free,'* F. F. Bruce notes that Nero did not likely hear Paul's case. "According to Tacitus, Nero announced at the beginning of his position as Caesar, *he would not judge cases in propria persona* (Latin for 'in one's own proper person')' as his predecessor Claudius had done also, and indeed, during his first eight years as Emperor, he generally delegated those tasks to others.[380]

There are no writings or records as to what 'Paul was up to' while he was waiting to 'stand before Caesar' or his principate; he did continually welcome visitors to his quarters so he might impart the Gospel, and Paul did continue writing Epistles. There are no Roman records as to Paul's disposition with the court. An important fact was Paul was not chained with only one guard. I cannot imagine Paul being held back for any length of time without 'anything happening.' There are other sources stating Paul may have gone on new missions to Crete, Asia Minor and Greece, but this is speculation. There is little, or no mention of a mission to Spain.

Chapter 15 Study Questions

1. What effect did Paul's appearance in Rome have on the Roman church in regards to his new Gospel?

2. How did the Roman Jews and Christians view Paul's message?

3. Did Paul make it to Spain?

---

[380] F. F. Bruce, p. 366.

Chapter 16

PAUL'S CAPTIVITY EPISTLES-EPHESIANS, PHILIPPIANS COLOSSIANS, PHILEMON

During the time of writing these four Epistles, Paul refers to himself as a prisoner, or "in bonds."[381] Theologians and academics refer to these letters as the 'prison epistles.' Paul was not physically in prison but was in detention (house arrest) in Rome. Other sources have mentioned Caesarea as the location from which Paul wrote the Epistles as he was imprisoned in that city for two years.[382] The term *captivity* more accurately expresses Paul's condition as he wrote these letters. Paul was awaiting trial and had the freedom to welcome visitors into his residence in Rome.

Many researchers and scholars also believe that Ephesians, Colossians, and Philemon were written while Paul was in Ephesus, possibly under arrest for some unknown reason. This hypothesis is not mentioned in Acts.

Ephesians, Colossians and Philemon, as a group of letters were penned close to one another, AD 60-62. Philippians may have

---

[381] Stanley, *Life Principles Bible, Ephesians 6:20-21, Philippians 1:7, Colossians 4:17-18, Philemon 1:22-23.*

[382] F. F. Bruce, p. 360.

been written in AD 62 as in that letter, Paul's attitude and hope of release was more optimistic.

Ephesians

Ephesians was written from Rome (or Ephesus) during early AD 60 while Paul was in detention, possibly AD 61. References in Ephesians suggest that Tychicus, a friend and church elder, carried the letter to its destination.[383] Bible scholars have suggested *Ephesians* was originally written as a *'circular letter'* with Paul's hope the letter would circulate and be read to all church assemblies throughout Asia Minor where he had ministered.[384] Determining the precise purpose for which Paul wrote Ephesians is difficult to do. Many of Paul's letters were written to meet or address specific needs of a certain church.

Ephesians has a solemn, serious tone as it outlines the important practices and doctrines for believers to keep in mind. Paul did not aim his statements in the letter against false teachings. Ephesians is a treatise of Christian truth concerning the Christian church, Christian unity, and the idea that as a Christian, one needs to 'walk in the light' with Jesus Christ. The understanding of this truth is as necessary for the church today as it was in Paul's day. Live as Jesus lived, or at least make a best effort.

After listing the divine resources available for believers, Paul wrote that he prayed that his readers and listeners might grow in the knowledge of God.[385] He specifically wanted the Ephesians to understand the hope of their calling, the riches of God's inheritance for believers, and the greatness of the divine power available to believers.

---

[383] Stanley, *Life Principles Bible, Ephesians 6:21-22.*
[384] Callewaert, *The World of St. Paul, pp. 100-101.*
[385] Stanley, *Life Principles Bible, Ephesians 1:15-22.*

The mention of the divine power of God as revealed in Christ's resurrection led Paul to discuss the illustration of that power in the transformation of the believers from spiritual death to heavenly life.[386] In their pre-Christian state of mind and heart, the Ephesians were dead 'in sin,' were enslaved to evil, and were the objects of God's wrath.[387] Paul wanted them to know that *in Christ* they would receive divine mercy that made possible a life of "good works." The good works were not an option for believers; they were necessary. [388] 'Good works' was seen as a 'thank-you' to Christ for his gift of eternal life.

The experience of conversion applied to Gentiles as well as Jews.[389] Gentiles lived with hope as did Jews for three thousand years. In Christ they have been reconciled with God and are at peace with God.[390] Because of the experience of reconciliation, Gentiles and Jews became citizens of *God's kingdom.* They were considered members of God's family, and God was building their minds and heart into a holy temple for His habitation.[391]

The Gentiles were also heirs of God along with the Jews.[392] Through their faith in Christ, they would share in all the promises God had made available. This focused on Paul's specific mission to declare the Gospel to the Gentiles as he believed the Jews and Gentiles were equal in God's eyes if they accepted Jesus Christ as their Savior and the Messiah. He saw his work as a special stewardship entrusted to him in spite of the suffering to which it had led.[393] Paul believed his involvement in God's plan was an

---

[386] Ibid. Ephesians 2:1-10.

[387] Ibid. Ephesians 2:11-22.

[388] Ibid. Ephesians 2:4-10.

[389] Ibid. Ephesians 2:11-22.

[390] Ibid. Ephesians 2:4-7.

[391] Ibid. Ephesians 2:19-22.

[392] Stanley, *Life Principles Bible, Ephesians 3:6–7.*

[393] Ibid. Ephesians 3:2-13.

unspeakable privilege.[394] Paul prayed that the Ephesians would experience strength through the Holy Spirit and grasp the depth of God's love for them.[395] He assured them God was able to carry out His work more abundantly than could be imagined.[396]

The proclamation of the spiritual blessings led Paul to show believers how they should apply the blessing to their lives. In Chapters 4-through 6, Paul described the new life that God's blessing would produce within them. Paul outlined the new behavior toward one another expected of all believers. Christians were to put off their old, pre-conversion lifestyle, and practice truth, honesty, wholesome talk, kindness, and forgiveness with one another.[397] Again we see the same basic messages throughout Paul's Epistles; a good point is in the letter to the Galatians in Chapter 5:22-23 concerning the fruits of the Spirit.

- Paul demanded a 'new life' of believers before nonbelievers. Believers were to "walk in love, sexual purity, the light of holy behavior, and wisdom." The Holy Spirit would provide the spiritual dynamic for energizing these demands.[398]

- Paul taught this 'new life' revolutionizes the Christian home.[399] Husbands and wives were to practice mutual submission to each other; Paul appealed to husbands to love their wives *sacrificially*.[400]

---

394 Ibid. Ephesians 3:8-10.

395 Ibid. Ephesians 3:14-21.

396 Ibid. Ephesians 3:20-21.

397 Ibid. Ephesians 4:17-32.

398 Ibid. Ephesians 5:1-21

399 Ibid. Ephesians 5:22 – 6:9.

400 Ibid. Ephesians 5:30-33.

- Children are to obey their parents, and parents were to provide consistent discipline and instruction for the children.[401] Christian servants are to obey their owners from the heart, and the owners were to treat their 'slaves' with the confidence that the Lord would reward their mercy and compassion.[402]

Christians were engaged in an unending struggle against the adversary's (Satan's) deceit and treachery.[403] Paul urged his believers to put on all of "God's armor" and to live in a state of prayerful readiness.[404] Paul pointed out the role of Tychicus as the carrier of the letter. He offered peace, love and grace to all Ephesians.[405]

My conclusion is Paul was writing to the Ephesians to emphasize the meaning of "getting right with God." Theologians and researchers alike question an underlying purpose of the Ephesian Epistle. As in his letter to the Romans, Ephesians covers many topics, but he stops short of detailing his ideas of corrections.

Philippians

The city of Philippi was name after Philip II of Macedonia who around the year 400 BC seized the city for its valuable mines. In 200 BC, Philippi passed on to Roman control. In 42 BC Philippi was the site of a battle between the armies of Octavian (later, Augustus Caesar) and Antony, the latter who defeated the armies of Brutus and Cassius. In 31 BC Octavian defeated the army of Antony at Actium. Octavian settled many of his defeated opponents in Philippi and made the city a Roman colony.

---

[401] Stanley, *Life Principles Bible, Ephesians 6:1–4.*

[402] Ibid. Ephesians 6:7-9.

[403] Ibid. Ephesians 6:10-20.

[404] Ibid. Ephesians 6:10-11.

[405] Ibid. Ephesians 6:21-24.

Paul first visited Philippi during his second missionary journey. It was a city of so few Jews that justification for a synagogue to be built was nil. On the Sabbath, Paul attended a prayer meeting on the banks of a river where Lydia (Paul's first European convert[406]) and others responded to his message. Those who attended the prayer meeting were probably Jews or proselytes, and even pagans.

Paul's additional experiences in Philippi revealed the Roman and pagan character of the city. After Paul freed a slave girl from demonic possession, her owners charge Paul and Silas with teaching unlawful customs.[407] Paul and Silas were thrown in prison, but an earthquake at midnight set the stage for their freedom. The jailer was also converted as a result of these remarkable events.

On the day after the earthquake, the city magistrates sent word to the jailer to release Paul and Silas. Paul protested they had unlawfully jailed Roman citizens and insisted the magistrates personally come and escort Paul and Silas from the area. After receiving what amounted to a veiled apology from the magistrates, Paul and Silas left Philippi.

Philippians was written near or at the end of Paul's two-year detainment in Rome. The Philippian church sent *Epaphroditus* to Paul with a financial gift for the collection.[408] After recovering from a serious illness, Epaphroditus returned to Philippi. Paul sent a note of gratitude for the gift with this trustworthy friend.

On occasion, the church of Philippi was a 'bundle of troubles' for Paul apparently from the beginning. The assembly had shown a tendency toward disunity and contentiousness. Paul rebuked them for having this spirit, and encouraged them to practice humility in their relationships with one another.[409]

---

[406] Ibid. Acts 16:14, 15, 40.

[407] Stanley, *Life Principles Bible, Acts 16: 20-21*.

[408] Ibid. Philippians 2:25-30.

[409] Ibid. Philippians 3:1-6.

Philippi had been infiltrated by Judaizers who diluted, or added to, the requirements for salvation. In addition to rebuking the Judaizers, Paul used severe language to rebuke *a group of perfectionists* in the church.[410]

Another group displayed tendencies toward sensuality and materialism. Paul sent them a warning against their errors. Paul intended to help the church defend itself from such strong theological crosscurrents, both inside and outside.[411]

Paul's letter also was preparing the Philippians for his and Timothy's forthcoming visit to the church. Timothy shared with Paul a passionate concern for the welfare of the Philippian Christians.[412] Paul's expression of hope to see his Christian friends soon indicated his two-year detention in Rome may have been nearing its end.[413] [414] [415]

Colossians

The church in Colossae was one Paul had not established or visited during his missionary travels. The city of Colossae was located approximately eighty miles east of Ephesus in Asia Minor. During the era of Greek dominance, it was a city of prominence. By the Roman era, it had fallen into disarray as had many cities in the geographical area due to severe earthquakes.

Colossae was located near major trade routes between the eastern and western territories. With a multitude of people and cultures traveling through the area, there was exposure to different religions

---

[410] Ibid. Philippians 3:12-21.

[411] Ibid. Philippians 3:18-19.

[412] Ibid. Philippians 2:19-23.

[413] Callewaert, *The World of St. Paul, pp.180,181.*

[414] Bruce, *Paul: Apostle of the Heart Set Free, p. 299.*

[415] Polhill, *Paul and His Letters, pp.1158, 159,*

and philosophies, such as Jewish legalism, Greek speculation, and the mysticism of the Orient, to name a few. Along with differing philosophies came false teachings and heretics. *Asceticism,* the practice of severe self-discipline, was characteristic of the heresies plaguing the church in Colossae.[416] *Asceticism* imposed restrictions on the body and demanded abstinence from certain objects, foods, or practices.

False teachings involved, among other things, the worship of angels.[417] Perhaps a featured doctrine encouraged the worship of angels as intermediaries between the Highest God and the physical universe. The development of an angelic hierarchy was characteristic of a later Christian heresy know as *Gnosticism* (a heretical characteristic stressing the escape from this world through the acquisition of esoteric knowledge).

When Paul wrote the letter to the Colossian church, he had a visitor by the name of *Epaphras* who maybe considered the founder of the Colossian church.[418] Epaphras had likely heard Paul evangelizing during a stay in Ephesus. Epaphras, upon returning to Colossae started evangelizing and spreading the Gospel. Most of the members of the congregation were Gentiles, with few Jews. Some of the problems that were occurring in the church were apparently related to Jewish misunderstandings of the Gospel.[419]

In the letter to the Colossians, Paul emphasized the supremacy of Christ. This emphasis suggests that the false teachers undercut the Christology Paul advocated. He also warned against being deceived by human philosophy and empty human speculation without divine revelation. Some efforts had been made to impose Jewish practices on the Colossian believers such as circumcision,

---

[416] Stanley, *Life Principles Bible, Colossians 2:20-23.*

[417] Ibid. Colossians 2:18.

[418] Ibid. Colossians 1:7-8.

[419] Ibid. Colossians 2:16-17, 20-22.

dietary regulations, and religious festivals, among other heresies plaguing the church of Colossae.

The messages in the letter to the Colossians are important to Christians of every generation as they encounter the philosophies of their time in history. By examining Paul's efforts to redress the error of his time, we can learn how to grapple with wayward thinking in our time. When thinking falls out of step with God's ideas, we must allow God to correct our errors.

Paul also emphasized realities with *transcultural appeal.* Relationships between husbands and wives, parents and their children, employer and employees, should reflect the impact of our Christian commitment. Paul reminded the recipients of the Colossians Epistle these are very important relationships.[420]

Philemon

Of all of Paul's correspondences, the letter to Philemon is the most private. It may have been read to the people who attended meetings at Philemon's home church. Philemon who may have lived in Colossae was a slave owner from whom Onesimus (his slave) had fled. Speculation has it that Philemon had been converted during Paul's residence in Ephesus.

Onesimus had been sent on a task by Philemon. He ended up robbing Philemon (an unproven supposition) and did not return, i.e. a runaway slave. Somehow, Paul's and Onesimus's paths crossed, and Onesimus was converted. Paul found Onesimus a faithful Christian servant, but he refused to keep Onesimus with him illegally. Paul returned the 'runaway slave' to Philemon and requested him to receive "him as a brother."[421]

---

[420] Polhill, *Paul and His Letters, pp. 322-328.*
[421] Stanley, *Life Principles Bible, Philemon 1: 1-12.*

Paul further requested Philemon to receive his former runaway slave as he would have received Paul. Paul promised repayment of any debt Onesimus owed. Without making a specific request for the release of Onesimus, Paul was nevertheless confident that Philemon would do more than he asked of him.[422] Paul included a request that Philemon prepare him a guest room.[423] Paul concluded his letter with greetings and an expression of grace.[424]

The following two features of the letter make it of great value in New Testament study:

- First the letter provides an example of a Christian approach to the *social issue of slavery*. Attacking the institution forthright would have been futile. Paul, both in Philemon and Colossian 4:1 urged owners of slaves to treat their slaves with compassion.

- Paul *sounded no call* for slaves to rise in rebellion but desired to melt the resistance of slave owners and slaves with a lavish outpouring of Christian love. When a slave owner could refer to his slave as a *"brother in Christ,"* emancipation hopefully would not be far away.

Christianity thus established conditions that made it unlikely slavery would ever endure as an institution even though Paul (or any biblical author) ever outright condemned the institution as immoral.

Finally, the letter to Philemon presents an intimate, personal account of Paul. Paul appealed to Philemon's generosity and Christian love. In the body of the letter Paul appeals to Philemon

---

[422] Ibid. Philemon 1:17-21.

[423] Ibid. Philemon 1:22.

[424] Ibid. Philemon 1:25.

to demonstrate those same qualities on behalf of Onesimus.[425] He writes not so much as a theologian or Apostle to the Gentiles, but more as a Christian man applying the Gospel he embraced and preached. Starting with the salutation of Philemon, Paul writes as if he is writing to a best Christian friend.[426] His words show his integrity and his compassion for both Philemon and Onesimus.[427] [428] [429] [430]

Chapter 16 Study Questions

1. Paul's "captivity letters" are also known as "circular letters." What was the purpose of the circular letters, and which assemblies might they address?

2. There was a primary reason Paul wrote each 'captivity letter' to a specific church or assembly. What was the primary purpose in each Epistle?

3. What may have been Paul's thoughts on slavery?

---

[425] Polhill, *Paul and His Letters, p. 347.*

[426] Stanley, *Life Principles Bible, Philemon 1:7-9.*

[427] Ibid. Philemon 1:16.

[428] Calleweart, *The World of St. Paul. pp. 182-183.*

[429] Polhill, *Paul and His Letters, pp.346-349.*

[430] Stanley, "The Epistle of Paul the Apostle to Philemon," *LIFE PRINCIPLES BIBLE, pp. 1449-1451.*

Chapter 17

THE PASTORAL EPISTLES

None of Paul's letters are more reflective of his pastoral orientation than the group known appropriately as the Pastoral Epistles, consisting of 1 & 2 Timothy, and Titus. These Epistles are devoted to matters of church organization (ecclesiastical discipline). "Paul is not offering the mellow thoughts of an 'armchair theologian;' he is writing passionate, urgent letters to assemblies facing immediate decisions that will affect every aspect of the members lives at work, at home, in the market square."[431] The Pastoral Epistles form a natural group among the Pauline letters. They were addressed to individuals rather than church assemblies, although their concerns were issues that involved entire congregations or assemblies. Paul may have intended Timothy and Titus to share the letters with their larger assemblies. The Pastoral Epistles are church and assembly letters in the sense that they address Timothy's and Titus's roles as congregational leaders.

Paul was a 'church planter with a pastor's heart.' One should not conclude this when Paul built a church it was built of brick, stone, and mortar. The idea of a church was more a congregation of people (an assembly) coming together in the Spirit of Jesus Christ – the Body of Christ.

---

[431] Robin Griffith-Jones, *The Gospel According to Paul (New York; HarpeCollins, 2015), p. 35.*

From the time of Paul's first mission, he made it his practice to revisit the congregations he established to make sure the churches had stable leadership. These letters, another means of maintaining contact with the churches, were read to the congregations, as they were often preoccupied with pastoral concerns.

During Paul's second mission he traveled through Ephesus with Timothy and learned the church was facing great spiritual difficulty. After a period of ministry, Paul departed leaving Timothy in charge.

Paul proceeded to Macedonia where he wrote First Timothy. As he wrote, he may have reflected on the role of Titus in Crete. First Timothy and Titus must have been written close together. Paul's mood in Second Timothy differs from that in the other two Pastoral Epistles. His personal struggles and mind-set due to imprisonment may be reflected in the letter.

The Pastoral Epistles form a closely related group and are so different from one another that many scholars deny Paul wrote them, but no early Christian writer ever questioned Paul's authorship. However, scholars in the nineteenth and twentieth centuries hinted at denying Paul's authorship, as Paul may have used an *amanuensis* with these Epistles – a person who could take dictation such as a secretary. This is a scholarly argument that has continued through the years, questioning vocabulary and style. It has been noted that arguments against Pauline authorship based solely on matters of wording and style do not carry weight because of Paul's use of co-authors and amanuenses. *Paul and His Letters* by John B. Polhill is an excellent reference on the understanding of the debate.[432]

Assuming Pauline authorship of the Pastoral Epistles, we must place the letters in the 'shadowy period of his life (AD 62 and

---

[432] John B Polhill, "Timothy and Titus: Conduct in the Household of God," *Paul and His Letters, p.397.*

beyond).' Establishing an exact chronology and the facts of Paul's life in 'the shadowy period' is impossible to 'pin down' based solely on present knowledge and text. The exact nature of Paul's movements during this period is unknown. Paul likely wrote First Timothy from Macedonia. In Second Timothy, Paul is possibly captive for a second time.

After Paul's initial release from the first Roman imprisonment, he *'may'* have returned to the East for further ministry. On the island of Crete, Paul and Titus experienced a successful ministry (***another mission***) and then departed leaving Titus to complete the task of organizing and instructing the infant churches Paul and Titus had founded.

The apostle apparently is in Rome expecting his execution (between AD 62 and 64).[433] The Epistle to Titus indicated Paul had an extensive missionary tour in Crete.[434] Also, when Paul wrote to Titus, he had planned to remain in Nicopolis during the winter.[435]

It has never been established if Paul ever visited Spain. He may have returned to Asia Minor after being released from an initial imprisonment. Since Timothy and Titus cover similar subjects, one may conclude that Paul wrote these letters in close proximity of one another. Judging from the tone of the final letter, Paul may have been staring death in the face.[436]

---

[433] Stanley, *Life Principles Bible, 2 Timothy 4:6-8. 13-18.*
[434] Ibid. Titus 1:3.
[435] Ibid. Titus 3:12.
[436] Ibid. 2 Timothy 4:6-8.

First Timothy

Paul's personal words to Timothy suggest Paul was focused chiefly on meeting Timothy's pastoral needs.[437] Paul mentioned Timothy's selfless ministry. Paul had a "father-son" relationship with Timothy.[438] Timothy may well have shared with the entire assembly the advice and insight Paul provided, but the chief impact of the letter was meant for Timothy.

Paul urged Timothy to provide personal resistance to the false teachings in Ephesus, and to help Timothy follow his guidance, Paul included the identity of the false teachers and the nature of their doctrine. His insistence on maintaining standards for church leaders suggested that erring church leaders were among those who were helping spread disorder. False teachers urging dietary restrictions and asceticism[439] seemed to be influenced by Jewish thought in their interest in the law and displayed a type of mysticism with emphasis on a superior knowledge (Gnosticism).[440]

Paul wrote the Ephesian Christians suggesting them to live as members of "God's household, or family."[441] He was eager for them to present a committed lifestyle for others to imitate in order to provide a contrast with the corrupt, self-seeking actions of the false teachers.

Paul warned against apostasy (the abandonment or renunciation of their beliefs) and asceticism.[442] He urged church members to consistently demonstrate Christian behavior and encouraged the

---

[437] Stanley, *Life Principles Bible, 1 Timothy 1:18-19, 4:12-16*

[438] Polhill, *Paul and His Letters, p.406.*

[439] Stanley, *Life Principles Bible,1 Timothy 4:3.*

[440] Ibid. 1 Timothy 6:21-22.

[441] Ibid. 1 Timothy 3:15.

[442] Ibid. 1 Timothy 4:1-4.

members to take care of true widows and warned against greed and materialism.

Neither First Timothy nor either of the other Pastoral Epistles should be viewed as church 'organizational manuals.' "They have been viewed as a sort of handbook, laying down the discipline and regulations for the church and the qualifications for its various ministries"[443] Paul was not writing a text on church administration; rather, he was preparing Timothy to deal wisely with false teachers who were threatening the vitality and accomplishments of the Ephesian church.[444] [445] Paul had all the confidence in the world in Timothy. Paul, from the very beginning of his ministry, had to deal with false teachers, Judaizers, and non-believers. In this Epistle, Paul is passing along years and decades worth of instructional text that would be a huge assistance for Timothy and Titus.

Second Timothy

Though it is not known exactly where Timothy was living when he received Paul's second letter, it was likely Ephesus. Paul's mood in Second Timothy was deeply influence by his personal circumstances. Speculation has Paul had been arrested for a second time and expected to be executed for unspecified reasons (AD 64-65). Paul felt very alone during this period as many of his friends had left on specific ministries leaving him without close associates.

The false teaching in the Ephesian church continued to spread. The church leader, Hymenacus and Alexander, excommunicated in First Timothy 1:20 continued to exert their evil influence on the church, and they had reinforcements.[446]

[443] Polhill, *Paul and His Letters, p. 407.*

[444] Polhil. pp. 397-406

[445] Stanley, *Life Principles Bible, "Introduction to the Book of First Timothy," Life Principle Bible, p.1428.*

[446] Ibid. *2 Timothy 2:17-18.*

Paul dealt with the heresy but was not preoccupied with it. He chose to focus his attention on Timothy. Paul reminded Timothy of their lengthy friendship and insisted that he be loyal to Paul's teachings and practice.[447]

Paul urged Timothy to focus his efforts on developing faithful followers of Christ. Paul appealed to Timothy to come to his side. Paul courageously faced the future and prepared Timothy to continue the work in his ministry even in the eventuality of Paul's death. Despite the circumstances in which Paul found himself, he encouraged suffering for the Gospel.[448] His words add a dimension of reality to the issue of suffering for Christians who lived in the West with little to fear vis-à-vis governmental persecution.

Martyrdom is still all too real for Christians in the Middle East and Asia Minor today including Syria, Turkey, Egypt, Afghanistan, and Africa. Paul's words are an encouraging example for those who might face the possibility of being martyred. Paul's images of discipleship show that its cost to the believer could be high.[449] He compares Christian commitment to the dedication of a soldier, an athlete, and a hardworking farmer and prepared Timothy for the cost of his commitment.[450]

Paul's words should remind us that, although salvation is free, the believer's response to salvation *demands commitment and endurance*. Throughout First Timothy, Paul appealed to Timothy to show courage, stamina and continuing commitment to proper doctrine. He urged Timothy to show loyalty despite the hardships he faced. He also encouraged Timothy to understand the truths that promote efficient ministry: "primarily, Jesus Christ is God's resurrected Son and Messiah."[451]

---

[447] Ibid. 2 Timothy 1:13-14, 2:1-13.

[448] Ibid. 2 Timothy 1:8

[449] Ibid. 2 Timothy 2:3-7

[450] Stanley, *Life Principles Bible, 2 Timothy 2:20-21.*

[451] Ibid 2 Timothy 2:8-13.

Paul wrote about the hardships he endured in assisting God's people in obtaining their salvation reminding 'Timothy was to copy him in maintaining an unrelenting purpose.' He reminded Timothy of the certainty of reward from God for faithful living. Paul concluded the Epistle with a personal greeting to his faithful friends Priscilla and Aquila, sharing information with Timothy about mutual friends and sending greetings to Timothy for other Christians in the Ephesian church.

Titus

Paul had left Titus on Crete to work through the difficulties in Christian churches. In his letter to Titus, he identified the qualifications of the elders or overseers of the church.[452] The Cretan church needed mature, upright leaders to combat the deceitful, stubborn opponents they faced in the false teachers.[453] Driven by a desire for personal gain and power, these false teachers were spreading widely and randomly, their errors which consisted primarily of "Jewish myths and adherence to Jewish law."[454]

Paul urged Titus to teach the older men to persevere in upright living, and the older women to be worthy examples for the younger women. Titus was to teach the younger men to show self-control in every area of life. Finally, Titus was to urge slaves to be obedient to their owners and to work honestly in order to make a Christian lifestyle attractive to all.

Paul then named three factors for Titus that inspired committed Christian living as follows:

---

[452] Ibid. Titus 1:5-9.

[453] Ibid. Titus 1:10-16.

[454] Ibid. Titus 1:14.

- The grace of God, a knowledge of divine grace promoting not carelessness but disciplined self-controlled living,

- The blessed hope of Christ's return as the knowledge of Christ's return provides an incentive for alert commitment to Christ,

- The position of Christians as God's special people as recognition of this special relationship should motivate believers to be eager to love, trust, praise, and obey God.[455]

In the third chapter of Titus, Paul began with an insistence on Christian submission to governmental authorities and an emphasis on considerate conduct toward all people. He suggested that the kindness and love of God in rescuing Christians from an aimless existence should produce full commitment. Finally, he focused on the renewal authored by the Holy Spirit; this regeneration being a source of strength for holy living.[456] Paul was encouraging Titus to encourage his assemblies to place God 'as number one' in their lives. If they followed this directive, they would find fewer trials and tribulations in their lives and times. Happy and encouraged people seem to be more inclined to practice their faith in Jesus Christ; *something that Paul knew and experienced.*

To recap, Paul's first and foremost goal in writing the Pastoral Epistles was not to give these new congregations a *'how-to manual on the everyday running of their churches.'* Titus and Timothy were by far two of the closest friends and confidants Paul had met and mentored throughout his second and third missions. I don't think for a moment that Paul wrote the letters to Timothy and Titus to question their faith or their knowledge of faith. He wanted them to remember to "stick to the program and Gospel as he had taught it."

---

[455] Stanley, *Life Principles Bible, Titus 2:13-15.*
[456] Ibid. Titus 3:5-7.

Paul was also very aware of the importance of getting and receiving the *'right people at the right time'* for the job. He seemed to have had a sixth sense in choosing *'the right people at the right time.'* Timothy and Titus are prime examples. Another is Phoebe, a successful businesswoman in Corinth whom Paul entrusted with delivering his Roman Epistle to the church in Rome.

Christianity was in its infancy, and it was competing with centuries-old pagan religions, not to mention the non-believers and Jews who would not accept the Gospel as Paul preached it. Paul wanted to keep his message intact (down to the letter) as it *has* remained other than in various modern-day translations of the Bible.

Chapter 17 Study Questions

1. Paul was blessed with good associates during his missions. Name any five of these associates and mention how they were associated with Paul.

2. Are Paul's messages to Timothy and Titus as relevant to our current church leaders as it was to them in that era? How?

Chapter 18

"TO DIE IS GAIN"

As St. Paul the Apostle is the *third and final* re-edited version of ***St. Paul: The Right Man at the Right Time***, I found it three-times more difficult to end my discussion and journey through the very remarkable life and times of St. Paul the Apostle. This work has been a joyful, life and spiritual altering experience – a labor of love.

In this edition there were new sources, authors, biblical scholars and theologians who presented theories concerning the time of Paul's death, and how he may have spent his final years. The study and research into Paul's life continues as there are still many unanswered questions.

Many modern scholars believe Paul died as a martyr during the reign of Nero, possibly in AD 67-68. Rome was burned in AD 64. Nero, from historical accounts was psychotic, a pedophile, and may have had the fires set to clear land for a new palace, and conveniently blamed the fires on the Jews and Christians. If Paul had made-it to Spain and returned only to be arrested a second time, this may have occurred between AD 64 and AD 66 (scholars, researchers and academics are of the opinion, Paul never traveled to Spain). St. Peter was martyred – crucified upside down in AD 64 while in Rome.

178

St. Peter, as in possibly the case of St. Paul, may have been imprisoned at the traditional site of the *Mamertine Prison* adjacent to the Roman forum. The prison was known for its horrible conditions, and those who entered usually did not come out alive. Prisoners were lowered into a hole that bottomed-out into two large cells; some refer to it as a 'sewer of Rome.' Men who found themselves incarcerated at this prison were to be brought to trial. In some cases, the prisoners were 'simply allowed to starve to death - out of sight.' Both men died at the hands of the Romans which is another indicator Paul may have died earlier than AD 67 or 68.

Paul's Final Resting Place

James D. Tabor, PhD, chairs the Department of Religious Studies at the University of North Carolina at Charlotte and has been a lifelong student of Paul. Tabor, in his book *Paul and Jesus – How the Apostle Transformed Christianity*, wrote an essay detailing his trip to Rome in May 2010 to finalize the research on his book titled *Paul and Jesus* and tried to demystify Paul's death and possibly pinpoint Paul's final resting place; the information below is an excerpt from his book:

> "For Tabor, the trip was a very personal pilgrimage in his lifelong study of St. Paul. The purpose was to visit the newly discovered tomb of Paul at the Basilica San Paolo, or St. Paul's Outside the Walls, one of the four major papal basilicas and the second largest next to St Peter's.
>
> At the end of 2006. Vatican archeologists announced they had unearthed an ancient stone sarcophagus, dated to the fourth century AD just below the central altar of the basilica and containing what they believed to be the skeletal remains of Paul. The sarcophagus was

inscribed *Paulo Apostolo Mart, Latin for 'Paul Apostle Martyr.'*

Traditions says Paul was beheaded during the reign of Emperor Nero at the spot now identified as Tre Fontane, at the end of the Via Laurentina. He was then buried two miles north along the Ostian Way, the ancient road from Rome to the Port of Ostia on the Mediterranean Sea.

The basilica was built over a cemetery that had been dated to the second century AD. In 324 AD, Emperor Constantine built a small basilica at the site to receive pilgrims visiting Paul's tomb.

On June 29, 2009, marking the traditional anniversary of Paul's death, Pope Benedict XVI announced that carbon-14 dating tests had been conducted on the skeletal remains inside the sarcophagus. The scientists had drilled a tiny hole in the sarcophagus, allowing them to access a small sample of skeletal remains as well as fabric. The tests on the bones confirmed a date from the first century or early second century AD."

As a lifelong student of St. Paul, Tabor found the visit to be profoundly meaningful. Kneeling in front of the tomb, surrounded by devoted pilgrims and curious visitors, he was deeply moved. Somehow the physical proximity to what may likely be Paul's earthly remains marked a milestone to a 45-year search for the historical Paul.

My hope is you believe as I do, 'St. Paul will live in our hearts and minds as- long as men, women, and children study the Old and

New Testaments; the latter including the Epistles of Paul.' Trying to get to know Paul on a personal level through speculation and conjecture in hundreds of books and studies, has been a delightful, consuming challenge; it is work that will continue.

Through the words of Paul's Epistles, and the repetitiveness of information found in many works, one gets a good sense of Paul's relentlessness regarding his expressed beliefs and faith in his Lord and Messiah, Jesus Christ. Paul was purpose driven and had an ironclad, fearless, never wavering belief system. Reasons as to why believers were drawn to him during his life and are still drawn to him include the following:

- His unwavering belief in God and Jesus Christ,

- His love of fellow Christians, new believers and new church assemblies,

- His desire to stay 'in touch' with his closest associates to ensue new believers were getting the correct doctrine and messages (as he saw it) of the Gospel of Jesus Christ and God's grace, forgiveness, salvation and holiness.

Paul's one deepest and most anguishing regrets was he could not convince many of his fellow Jews the Lord Jesus Christ was the fulfillment of the Psalms, the Prophets, the Torah and the promises from scriptures of the Prophets in the Old Testament. Paul believed Jesus Christ was the True Messiah he had been waiting for ever since he, his mother and father had attended the synagogue and heard of a Messiah appearing, possibly from the Davidian lineage. Time will tell as to what Paul believed was true. I believe most Christians and believers in our modern day will concur St. Paul, the Apostle to the Gentiles was *'The Right Man at the Right Time. Amen. 12-22-2021*

PAUL'S MISSIONARY JOURNEYS MAPS

"Maps reproduced from Bible Atlas & Companion, ©2008 by Barbour Publishing, Inc., use by permission all maps created by David Barrett(www.Biblemapper.com) Satellite terrain imagery produced with data provided by Global Land Cover Facility, http://www.landcover.org. Author: MDA Federal 2004. Landstar GeoCover 2000/ETM + Edition Mosaics, Sioux Falls, South Dakota: USGS. All elevation data was created from data supplied by Shuttle Radar Topography Mission (SRTM, a project of NASA). A full description of this data can be found at http://www.USGS. gov."

ROME AT TIME OF PAUL

PAUL'S FIRST MISSION

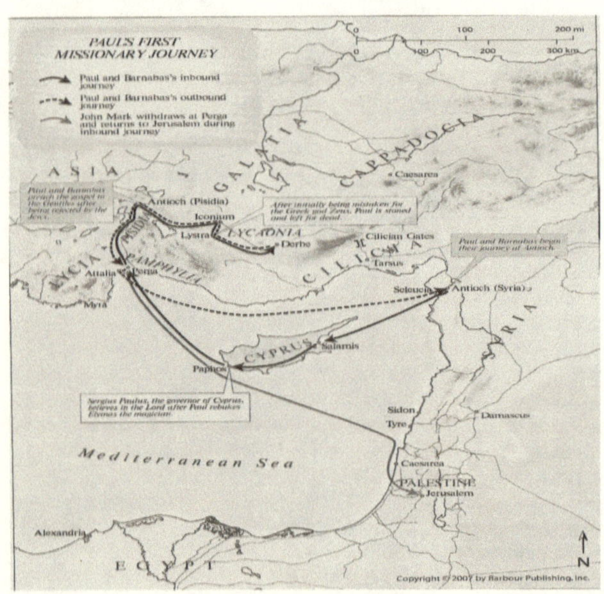

PAUL'S SECOND MISSION

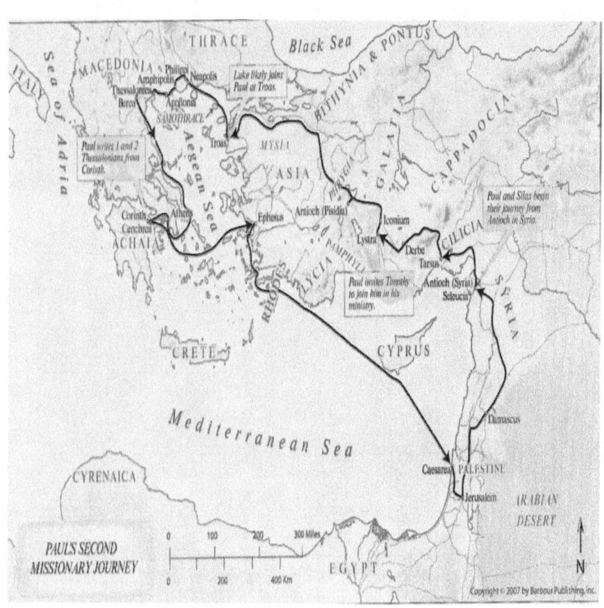

PAUL'S THIRD MISSION

PAUL'S FINAL MISSION

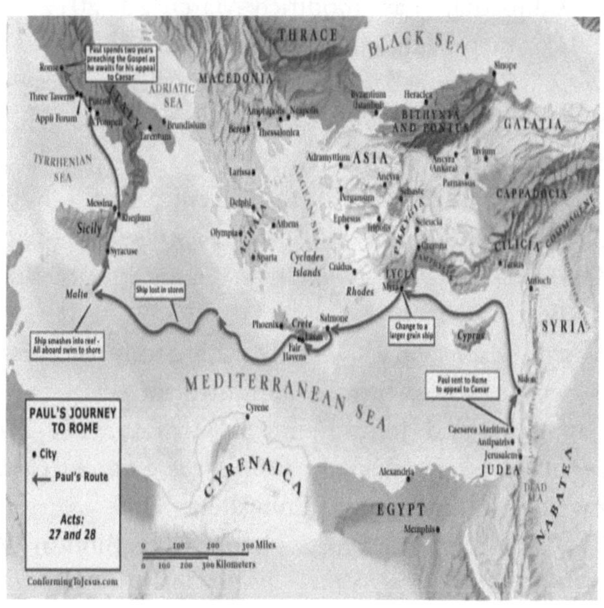

BIBLIOGRAPHY

"*Antonius Felix*," Wikipedia. Last modifies March 14, 2017. Accessed April 4, 2017. https://en.wikipedia.org/wiki/Antonius_Felix.

"*Apollos*," Wikipedia. Last modified March 20, 2017. Accessed April 3, 2017. https://en.wikipedia.org/wiki/Apollos.

"*Athenodorus Canaites*," Encyclopedia Britannica. Last modified April 4, 2017. www.britannica.com/biography/Athenodorus-Canaites.

Barton, Bruce B., Philip W. Comfort, Kent Keller, Linda Chaffee Taylor, and David R. Verman. "*Bible Commentary – Ephesians,*" In *Life Application: Bible Commentary.* Carol Stream, IL: Tyndale House Publications, 1996.

Blank, Wayne. "*Antiochus IV.*" Daily Bible Study. Acccessed April 5, 2017. www.keyway.ca/htm2002/antoiv.htm.

Borg, Marcus J., and John Dominic Crossan, *The First Paul: Reclaiming the Radical Visionary Behind the Church's Conservative Icon.* New York: HarperCollins Publishers, 2009.

Briggs, C. W., "*The Apostle Paul In Arabia,*" The Biblical World 41, no.4 (April 1913): p. 255-259.

Brittle, Irving L. Jr., *It's Not Rocket Science – The Theology of St. Paul.* New York, N.Y., Global Summit House Publishing, November, 2021

Bruce, F. F., *Paul: Apostle of the Heart Set Free*, Carlisle, Cumbrian: Paternoster Press, 1977.

Callewaert, Joseph M., *The World of St. Paul.* Translated by Michael J. Miller, San Francisco: Ignatius Press, 2006.

'Cleopatra's Gate in Tarsus,' turkisharchaeonews.net/object/cleopatras-gate-tarsus, accessed Nov. 14, 2019.

Cole, Dan P., "*Corinth and Ephesus: Why Did Paul Spend Half His Journeys in the Cities?*" December 1988. Accessed April 3, 2017. Biblical Archeology Society (BAS Library), Review 4.6.

"*Corinth in the Bible.*" Bible History Online. Accessed April 3, 2017. www.bible-history.com/isbe/c/CORINTH.

Crane, Frank, "*Letters of Pilate to Herod,*" *Lost Books of the Bible and the Forgotten Books of Eden* (Newfoundland: World Bible Publishers, 1926), p. 276.

Dockery, David S., *Concise Bible Commentary*. Nashville: B & H Publishing, 1998, 2010.

Douglas, J. D., and Merrill C. Tenney. *NIV Compact Dictionary of the Bible*, Grand Rapids, MI: Zondervan, 1989.

Dunn, James D. G. *The Theology of Paul the Apostle*. Grand Rapids MI: William B. Eerdmans Publishing Company, 2006.

------, *The New Perspective on Paul*. Grand Rapids, MI; William B. Eerdmans Publishing Company, 2008.

------, *Jesus, Paul and the Gospels*. Grand Rapids, MI: William B. Eerdmans Publishing Company, 2011.

Eason, Stephen P. "*Fruit of the Spirit.*" June 26, 2016. Accessed April 3, 2017. First Presbyterian Church, Richmond, VA. www.fpcrichmond.org.

------, "*Twelve Words, of Hope for the World: Freedom.*" July 2, 2017. First Presbyterian Church, Richmond, VA. www.fpcrichmond.org/sermons.

"*Eusebius Pamphilius.*" Accessed April 4, 2017. The Preterist Archive. www.preteristarchive.com/ChurchHistory/0325_eusebius_history.html.

"*Extra-Biblical Evidence Regarding Paul, Translation of 1 Clement 5:5-7.*" August 2012. https://memoirandremains.wordpress.com/2012/08/15/extra-biblical.

Fairchild, Mark R. "*Why Perga? Paul's Perilous Passage through Pisidia.*" November-December 2013. Accessed April 3, 2013, 2013 BAS Library, review 39.6. https://www.baslibrary.org/biblical-archeology-review/39/6/5.

"*Festus.*" Wikipedia. Last modified February 26, 2017. Accessed April 4, 2017. https://en.wikipedia.org/wiki/Porcius_Festus.

Furnish, Victor Paul. *"Corinth in Paul's Time – What Can Archeology Tell Us?"* May/June 1998. Accessed April 9, 2017. Biblical Archeology Society (BAS Library), review 14:3. http// www.basliibrary.org/biblical-archeology-review 14/3/1.

"Gamaliel." The Latter Rain Page. Accessed April 1, 2017. www. latter-rain.com/train/gama.htm.

"Gospel Principles." The Church of Jesus Christ of Latter-Day Saints. Salt Lake City, 1978, 2009.

Griffith-Jones, Robin. *The Gospel According to Paul.* New York: HarperCollins Publishers, 2004.

"Halakha." Wikipedia. Last Modified December 31, 2015. Accessed April 15, 2017. https//en.wikiquote.org/wiki/Halakha.

"Herod Agrippa II." Wikipedia. Last modified January 31, 2017, https://en.wikipedia.org/wiki/Herod_Agrippa_II.

Hill, Bryan. *"The Infamous Mamertine Prison and the Supposed Incarceration of Saint Peter."* July 19, 2015. Accessed April 21, 2017. Ancient Origin. http://www.ancient-origins.net/ancient-places-europe/infamous-mamertine-prison-and-supposed-incarceration-saint-peter-003447.

"Hillel the Elder." Wikipedia. Last modified January 23, 2017. Accessed April 3, 2017. https://en.wikiquote.org/wiki/ Hillel_the_Elder.

Hodge, Charles. *Romans.* Edited by Alister McGrath and J. I. Packer. Wheaton. IL: Crossway Books, 1993.

Hudson, David Christopher and Todd Bolen. *Bible Atlas and Companion*, Uhrichsville, OH: Barbour Publishing, 2008.

Ironside, H. A. *An Ironside Expository Commentary: Romans and Galatians.* Grand Rapids, MI: Kregel Publications, originally published 1928 and 1941, reprinted 2006.

------, *An Ironside Commentary: 1 & 2 Corinthians.* Grand Rapids, MI: Kregel Publications, originally published in 1938, reprinted 2006.

"John Hyrcanus I." Encyclopedia Britannica. Last Updated July 20, 1998. Accessed April 10, 2017. www.britannica.com/biography/John-Hyrcanus-I.

Father Jerome. *"Paul," in De Viris Illustribus*, 646.

Josephus, Flavius. *The Works of Josephus.* Translated by William A. M. Whiston. Peabody, MA: Hendrickson Publishers, 1987.

"Juvenal, Roman Satirist." About.com.

"Kione Greek." Wikipedia. Last modified April 3, 2017. Accessed April 3, 2017. https//en.wikipedia.org/wiki/Kione_Greek.

Kroll, Woodrow. *The Book of Romans – Righteousness in Christ.* Chattanooga: Tyndale Theological Seminary, AMG Publishers, 2002.

Lea, Thomas D. and David Alan Black. *The New Testament: Its Background and Message.* Nashville: B & H Publishing Group, 2003.

"Letter of Tears." Wikipedia. Last modified March 30, 2017. Accessed April 9, 2017. https://en.wikipedia.org/wiki/Second_Epistle_to_the_Corinthians.

Lockyer, Herbert. *All the Apostles of the Bible.* Grand Rapids, MI: Zondervan, 1972.

"Lycaonia." Wikipedia. Last Modified February 27, 2017. Accessed April 2, 2017. https://en.wikipedia.org_Lycaonia.

Mack, Burton I. *Who Wrote the New Testament?* New York: HarperCollins, 1995.

Maier, Paul, translated. *Eusebius: The Church History*, Grand Rapids, MI: Kregel Publications, 2007.

McGee, J. Vernon. *Through the Bible Commentary Series: The Epistles – Romans Chapters 1 – 8 and 9 – 16.* Nashville: Thomas Nelson Publishing, 1991.

Mendels, Doron. *"Why Paul Went West: The Differences Between the Jewish Diasporas."* January- February 2011. Accessed April 19, 2017. Biblical Archaeology Society (BAS Library), review 37:1. http://www.baslibray.org/biblical-archaeology-review 37/1/10.

Miller, Adam W. *An Introduction to the New Testament.* Anderson, IN: Warner Press, 1972.

Murphy-O'Conner, Jerome. *"On the Road and On the Sea with St. Paul."* Sidebar: *"The Second Missionary Journey of Paul."* Summer 1985. Accessed April 4, 2017. Biblical Archaeology Society (BAS Library). Review 1:2. http://wwwbaslibrary.org/bible-review/1/2/8.

------. *"What Was Paul Doing in Arabia?"* October 1994. Accessed April 10, 2017. Biblical Archaeology Society (BAS Library), review, 10:5. http://www.baslibrary.org/bible-review/10/5/8.

New American Standard Bible. Copyright 1960. 1962, 1963, 1968, 1971, 1975, 1977, 1995 by Lockman Foundation.

Osteen, Joel. *Break Out.* New York: Faith Works Hachette Book Group, 2013.

Pagels, Elaine. *Revelations, Visions, Prophecy and Politics in the Book of Revelation.* New York: Viking Press, 2012

Phillips, John. *Exploring Romans: An Expository Commentary.* Grand Rapids, MI: Kregel Publications, 1969.

"Phoebe (Biblical Figure)," Wikipedia. Last modified March 12, 2017. Accessed April 21, 2017. https://en.wikipedia.org/wiki/Phoebe_(Christian_woman).

Polhill, John B. *Paul and His Letters*, Nashville: B&H Publishing, 1999.

"Ritual Purifications." Wikipedia. Last modified April 2, 2017. Accessed April 4, 2017. https://en.wikipedia.org/wiki/Ritual_Purification.

"Roman Citizenship." Wikipedia. Last modified January 25, 2017. Accessed April 10, 2017.https://en.wikipedia.org/wiki/Roman_citizenship.

"Saint Peter." Wikipedia. Last modified April 1, 2017. Accessed April 4, 2017. https://en.wikipedia.org/wiki/Saint_Peter.

"Second Epistle to the Corinthians." Wikipedia. Last modified March 30, 2017. Accessed April 13, 2017. https://en.wikipedia.org/wiki/Second_Epistle_to_the Corinthians.

"Seneca the Younger." Wikipedia. Last modified March 29, 2017. Accessed April 3, 2017. https://en.wikipedia.org/wiki/Seneca_the_Younger.

"Sepphoris – The Great City in Lower Galilee." Bible History Outline. Accessed April 10, 2017. www.bible-history.com/sites/Sepphoris.html.

"Shammai." Wikipedia. Last modified March 23, 2017. Accessed April 23, 2017. https://en/wiki.org/wiki/Shammai.

"St. Paul at Athens." HTDB/AGS Consulting. Accessed April 4, 2017.www.agsconsulting.com/hrdbv5/r5918.htm.

Stanley Charles F. *Life Principles Bible.* *New American Standard Bible.* La Habra, CA: Lockman Foundation, 2009.

Tabor, James D. *The Jesus Dynasty.* Hammersmith, London: Simon & Schuster and Harper Element, 2006.

------, *Paul and Jesus: How the Apostle Transformed Christianity.* New York: Simon & Schuster, 2012.

"Veria." Wikipedia. Last modified February 4, 2017. Accessed April 4, 2017. https://en.wikipedia.org/wiki/Veria.

Walker, Margaret, ed. *Paul: Jewish Law and Early Christianity.* Biblical Archeology Society Edition.

Williams, Adam W. *Brief Introduction to the New Testament.* New York: Pyramis Books, 1972.

Willis, Garry. *What Paul Meant.* New York: Penguin Books, 2006.

Wilson, A. N. *Paul: The Mind of the Apostle.* New York: W. W. Norton, 1997.

Wright, N. T. *Paul for Everyone: The Prison Letters – Ephesians, Philippians, Colossians, and Philemon.* Minneapolis: Fortress Press, 2002.

Wright, N. T., *Paul and the Faithfulness of God, Parts III and IV.* Minneapolis: Fortress Press, 2013.

Wright, Tom. *Paul For Everyone: Part One, Chapters 1-8.* Louisville: Westminster John Knox Press, 2004.